The drama classroom

The Drama Classroom provides an accessible and manageable approach for educators wanting to teach drama activities in educational, vocational and community settings. Informed by the pioneering work of the Brazilian educator, Paulo Freire, the text claims that drama educators work most effectively when they reflect on and in practice.

Clear advice is provided on what the key elements and principles are for effective drama practice. Informed by international developments in the teaching of drama, *The Drama Classroom* incorporates the pioneering work of two leading educators. Cecily O'Neill's emphasis on pre-text, or how educators need to weave challenging material into the introductory phases of drama activity is analysed. David Booth's approach to storydrama, and how such can be used as an effective learning medium across the curriculum is examined. The text blends good theory and practice (praxis) and demonstrates how educators can become effective reflective practitioners in drama education. Pitched for all levels, primary, secondary and tertiary, *The Drama Classroom* is a necessary and relevant resource for those committed to the power of drama in education.

Philip Taylor is Director of the Centre for Applied Theatre Research at Griffith University, Brisbane, Australia. He is well known for his work in teacher research and reflective practice in drama education and a regular presenter at conferences worldwide. His previous books include *Redcoats and Patriots: Reflective Practice in Drama and Social Studies* and *Researching Drama and Arts Education: Paradigms and Possibilities* (Falmer Press).

The drama classroom:
Action, reflection, transformation

Philip Taylor

London and New York

First published 2000
by RoutledgeFalmer
11 New Fetter Lane, London EC4P 4EE

Simultaneously published in the USA and Canada
by RoutledgeFalmer
29 West 35th Street, New York, NY 10001

Reprinted 2001, 2002 by RoutledgeFalmer

RoutledgeFalmer is an imprint of the Taylor & Francis Group

Typeset in 10/14pt Melior by Graphicraft Limited, Hong Kong
Printed and bound in Great Britain by TJ International Ltd,
Padstow, Cornwall

British Library Cataloguing in Publication Data
A catalogue record for this book is available from the British Library

Library of Congress Cataloging in Publication Data
A catalogue record for this book has been requested

ISBN 0-750-70779-8

For two of my inspiring mentors in drama praxis,
Cecily and David

Contents

Acknowledgements

My thanks to Drama Australia and the Queensland Association for Drama in Education for permitting me to adapt for this text work I have previously presented for them. My gratitude to the Creative Arts Team at New York University for hosting my sabbatical in 1998 which enabled me to research this book, especially my sincere thanks to Lynda Zimmerman and Chris Vine.

Chapter 1

Drama praxis: elements and principles

Drama praxis: the three elements

Drama praxis refers to the manipulation of theatreform by educational leaders to help participants act, reflect and transform. At the core of drama praxis is the artful interplay between three elements – people, passion and platform – as leaders and participants strive towards aesthetic understanding.

People

Drama is a collaborative group artform where people transform, act, and reflect upon the human condition. In drama, people are the instruments of inquiry. Stanislavski, the great Russian theatre director, made this very clear. 'People', he suggested, 'generally do not know how to make use of the physical apparatus with which nature has endowed [them].' The physical self is at the centre of a dramatic encounter and students in drama should be educated in how best to manipulate their 'instrument' (Stanislavski, 1949, p. 35).

Shakespeare's character, Hamlet, is well aware of the critical role the human instrument plays when signing meaning. Hamlet's instructions to the players prior to the performance of 'The Murder of Gonzago' capture the skills the actors must bring to their parts:

> *Speak the speech, I pray you, as I pronounced it to you, trippingly on the tongue; but if you mouth it, as many of your players do, I had as*

lief the town-crier spoke my lines. Nor do not saw the air too much with your hand, thus; but use all gently: for in the very torrent, tempest, and, as I may say, the whirlwind of your passion, you must acquire and beget a temperance that may give it smoothness. O it offends me to the soul to hear a robustious periwig-pated fellow tear a passion to tatters . . .   (*Hamlet*, III. ii)

Yet, it is not only the physical self which signs meaning, the inner or psychological self needs equally to be understood, to be manipulated, if messages are to be successfully conveyed. If you like, participants in drama are split into two parts. Actors live, weep, and laugh on the stage, continues Stanislavski, but as they do so, they observe and control themselves in the action: 'It is this double existence, this balance between life and acting that makes for art' (p. 167).

Art in drama praxis is a conscious manipulation of people in time and space. This then leads on to the second key element, passion.

Passion

I am using the term passion to refer to a heightened state which can arouse strong and emotive responses. In drama, the passion refers to the fictitious world where the participants find themselves, a world which demands that people momentarily step into imagined roles, characters and situations. Shakespeare referred to his theatre as 'a fiction . . . a dream of passion' (*Hamlet*, II. ii). In the Christian liturgical year, the passion refers to the narrative of Christ's crucifixion. The passion, then, is the unfolding tale, the stories that contain, as Hamlet says, the 'abstracts and brief chronicles of the time' (II. ii) in which we live.

In his book *The Rainbow of Desire*, the South American theatre director Augusto Boal (1995), argues that theatre cannot exist without passion. He likens theatre to a passionate combat of two human beings on a platform. 'Theatre denotes conflict, contradiction, confrontation and defiance', he argues, quoting the work of the Spanish dramatist Lope de Vega (p. 16). Theatre is a passion, a heightened state which elevates and focuses attention to another plane.

For my purposes, I will broaden this definition to encompass the created world which people conspire to make, present and reflect upon. While the passion might involve 'combat', it does not always. I am attracted to the argument of the British educator Gavin Bolton, who was one of the first leaders to claim how clumsy the term 'conflict' can be when describing classroom drama. For Bolton, drama expresses the constraints upon the expression of a conflict. If we look at the features of theatreform, we note how often characters find themselves in situations where they are prevented from expressing who they are.

In Shakespeare's play, Hamlet is prevented from expressing his view that Claudius killed his father as he feels he needs more evidence and solicits the players' help in this endeavour. George and Martha in *Who's Afraid of Virginia Woolf* (Albee, [1962] 1965), are not able to accept through the play how they have created a fictitious child to stop them from confronting the kind of shallow lives they have constructed for themselves. The male characters in *The Weir* (McPherson, 1999), simultaneously, are not in conflict with one another in the play but rather are constrained by their life circumstances to express the kind of human beings they are and those they aspire to become. We can all think of other examples of where the heart of the drama is located in the situations that prevent truths being revealed. Often in drama, it is when the conflict between or within the characters is expressed, that the curtain comes down, and the play ends. The drama does not focus on the conflict between character, but the forces operating on character which inhibit or constrain the expression of conflict.

Platform

I am not referring here to a raised area where the passion is performed, although drama occurs on elevated physical platforms. I am referring to that marked space, what Boal describes as the aesthetic space, where people creating passions live. Such platforms, aesthetic spaces, can be in classrooms, on streets, in hospitals, business organisations. Throughout time, these spaces have been marked in a variety of ways: around campfires, on horse-drawn carriages, in fields. We know that in Elizabethan times, actors were pretty much strolling players performing their plays wherever they found a friendly audience. Sometimes, they would create platform spaces on the backs of their carts, although a much-yearned-for setting would be an inn yard where proximity between actors and spectators was intimate, and as Day (1996) argues, a setting later 'deliberately copied in the eventual design of the amphitheatres' (p. 6).

The formality of mainstream theatre houses is but one space in which passions can occur, perhaps the more conventional space, certainly from the time of Shakespeare. But the praxis contained within this book pushes the boundaries of those mainstream houses into a variety of vocational, community and educational settings: parks, street fairs, hospital wards, business training sites, police stations, conference venues.

What is common to the platform spaces, wherever they be, is that people and passions occur on them, and that audiences engage with them. In the drama classroom though, the audience can be the participants themselves as they work towards aesthetic understanding.

Aesthetic understanding

Aesthetic, a word which has confounded and perplexed commentators for some time, refers to how satisfying we find the dramatic work, how well it massages our senses. My colleague Maxine Greene,[1] the eminent American philosopher, argues that aesthetic education requires people to attend to artworks with discrimination and authenticity. And by that she refers to a capacity for people to understand how the form manipulates the content and vice versa.

In drama praxis then, we want our students to be able to manipulate the elements of their craft (people, passion and platforms), to understand how that manipulation works, so that audiences can appreciate and be transformed through the medium. And it takes a lot of understanding, argues Greene – understanding of how art conspires to generate meaning.

And the purposes of aesthetic understanding? Yes, there are the functional and communication skills which can be developed, and the social habits which can be refined, but these skills are not dependent on drama praxis, and there are other curriculum areas which deal with them. The reasons for drama praxis are the insights to be made, the revelations to be had. 'The play's the thing / Wherein I'll catch the conscience of the king (II. ii)', states Hamlet, fully aware of the power of the dramatic artform to raise levels of consciousness. It is vital that educators remember that the arts' role through the generations has been to 'chronicle the time', to unfold the nature of our lives and the world in which we live. If operated well, theatre can be a powerful educative medium.

Praxis not practice

For many years now, the word 'practice' has suggested something quite different from theory. Practice connoted the doing, the active, the process. Theory connoted the not-doing, the thinking about, the product. Unfortunately such words, theory and practice, led to unhealthy divisions between those who thought or wrote about drama compared with those who did and practised drama. The thinkers couldn't practise, and the practitioners weren't thinkers, or so the argument went. The word 'praxis', though, brings these two aspects of theory and practice together, seeing both as a part of a complex dynamic encounter.

We will see in Chapter 5 how damaging the separation of theory from practice can be, especially when those involved in theatre studies differentiated what they did from the work of drama educators. As we will read, a most peculiar distinction of drama from theatre was made, where those who did drama claimed they were involved in process-oriented modes, whereas those who did theatre were interested in the product. What such distinctions failed to take into account was that just as drama educators were equally interested in product, theatre workers were equally interested in process.

Those outside the field knew nothing of these divisions and found them confusing and odd when they heard about them. It is fair to say that such divisions have damaged the discipline, with neither the theatre studies people nor the drama educators benefiting. I well recall how rancour in the theatre and drama camps reached such a height that when I first commenced work at The University of Melbourne, Australia, the theatre staff were segregated from their drama colleagues by four floors. No wonder, some thought, the School in which both were housed has since disbanded. Those involved in theatre arts and drama education, the argument went, are not team players and don't get on (see O'Brien and Dopierala, 1994).

We who have a commitment to teacher education and curriculum reform, especially in the field of theatre education, are aware that many of the great practitioners are equally the great theorists. I am thinking of the brilliant educator Dorothy Heathcote (see Resources section, p. 134), perhaps the most talented practitioner of educational drama this past century. It would be unfair to describe her simply as one who practised drama, as her conceptual understanding of what drama was for, and how to implement it, has transformed generations of educators.

As well, I am reminded of Heathcote's contemporary Gavin Bolton, who, while he provided a theoretical framework for us to conceptualise drama, was a superb teacher himself, able to demonstrate ideas in action.[2] And there are many others.[3] Each of the field's leaders has a commitment to teacher education, a respect for its scholarship, and a shared interest in how to structure and investigate theatre in the curriculum. They cannot be simply labelled as practitioners or theoreticians, but bring together a blend of theory and the practice which informs it.

There are historical reasons why drama became the preferred term for identifying improvised theatre work which occurred predominantly in school classrooms, and I deal with these in Chapter 5. Needless to say, though, we are now recognising that while drama might have been an appropriate way of describing the practice of good teachers, the term did promote a division from theatre practice which we are still trying to unravel today.

I much prefer the term 'drama praxis' to 'drama practice'. Praxis, a word developed by the Brazilian educator Paulo Freire (1970), claims that at the heart of sound education is an ability to help teachers and their students reflect and act upon their world, and through that process transform it into something more equitable and worth while. Praxis is powered by an agenda, a desire to push us to reflect upon our own practices, refine our theoretical leanings, as a step towards acting on and changing our life circumstances. Put simply, praxis denotes the action, reflections and transformation of people as they engage with one another. And those involved in praxis can anticipate that such action, reflection and transformation should help people create a just and better world.

Drama praxis in the curriculum

Often educators can forget that drama praxis is characterised by an active and improvisational encounter controlled by a particular educational context. A problem with many curriculum guides is that they present objectives and content in a static and lifeless manner seemingly ignoring the fact that people have to make curriculum happen. Any good drama teacher knows that curriculum is a lived experience; it is negotiated with colleagues and students – a fallible event dependent upon the abilities, moods and backgrounds of those who construct it.

In my view, curriculum statements and profiles are tenuous documents when they focus on predetermined results and when they ignore that outcomes occur in process. Attainment targets or outcomes statements point to the end rather than the means. The distinguished American educator Elliot Eisner (1991), for example, tells us that knowing the outcome of the game tells us little about how it is played. In drama praxis we are concerned with the process of playing, and while we usually have goals and directions it is the immediate classroom context that shapes them. Curriculum documents rarely include this vital contextual component of the teachers, the students, and their respective school communities.

Teachers have to become quite adept at reading classroom context; students react differently on given days and the material they are presented with can raise passionate or lethargic responses which could never have been predicted. Research reveals that students have a strong investment in the development of curriculum; the students' aesthetic responses are driven by their own reading, or misreading, of a specific moment. The cultural, social, sexual and physiological make-up of a classroom context inevitably impacts on attitudes students reveal in drama. Teachers have a responsibility to recognise how understandings are constructed in process and how they can co-construct curriculum content and its implementation.

The following example of drama praxis is driven by group co-construction. While the plan is familiar to the teacher, in this case myself, I know that each group of participants will respond differently to the work. Although teachers may safely assume that there are conventional readings of the material, they also are aware that people's relationship to content is dependent on their own interpretation of the world. The example to follow is one of my own design which has been taught with primary, secondary and higher education students. The plan is a useful one for highlighting ten key principles of drama praxis which inform this book. These principles reinforce the lived experience of the encounter in drama praxis. For ease of reading, the curriculum principles will be located within the lesson's episodic sequence.

Reinventing the three little pigs: a drama about prejudice and stereotype

Good story books can be a powerful entry point into drama activity, particularly when they raise questions or suggest puzzlements. David Booth (1994), who coined the term 'storydrama' (see Chapter 3), has argued that puzzlements refer to fascinating, sometimes baffling, issues provoked by a text. This issue might be an unsolved problem, a dilemma encountered by a character, or a point of intrigue suggested by an action, a stance or a response. Drama praxis with children can explore the issues, events and relationships posed by stories. Rather than acting out plots, a phenomenon Americans liken to story dramatisation, storydrama is situated in its improvisational exploration and the understandings school groups generate with each story's puzzlement. In this respect, storydrama shares much in common with process drama (see Chapter 2) as both shift participants' perceptions through the experience of the dramatic artform.

The True Story of The Three Little Pigs by Jon Scieszka (1989) raises many different puzzlements for a variety of age groups – puzzlements focusing on stereotype, values, and people's blinkered perceptions. How are pigs and wolves considered in this world? To what extent do cultural understandings impact on our reading of events? How are judgements formed and when are they ill-conceived? These are three questions neatly evoked by the Scieszka story and which resonate with everyday dilemmas about attitude formation and people's morality system.

While the book humorously focuses on the wolf's version of what really happened when he tangled with the three little pigs, light-hearted entry points into drama can lead to provocative and challenging explorations. At the heart of storydrama is the evolving struggle which students encounter as they construe their own unique understanding of the world. Scieszka's tale provides the vehicle, or what Cecily O'Neill (1995) describes as the pre-text, through which blinkered perceptions of events, people and relationships can be exposed.

The plan

Episode 1: Telling the tale
The teacher is familiar enough with the Sciezska version that he can almost tell it verbatim without referring to the text. There are strong advantages in this ploy: eye contact is an important factor within the opening moments of structured improvisation. The teacher is drawing the students into the humour of the tale as the wolf, Alexander T. Wolf, recounts how his motives with the pigs were pure; he was merely attempting to get from them a cup of sugar for his grandmother's birthday cake. His nagging sinuses, however, led to havoc when he 'sneezed a great sneeze' and the first two pigs' poorly built houses were destroyed. The dead porkers, the wolf maintains in defence, are as tempting a food for him as cheese hamburgers are for humans. Readers might find an adapted version of the Scieszka tale helpful:

> *So you think you know the real story of the three little pigs. I'll let you in on a secret. Nobody knows the real story because I haven't told my side of the story. I'm the wolf. Alexander T. Wolf. I don't know how this whole big bad wolf thing got started. But it is all wrong. The real story is about a sneeze and a cup of sugar. This is the real story.*
>
> *Way back in fairy story time. I was baking a birthday cake for my dear old granny. I had a terrible sneezing cold and I ran out of sugar. So I thought I'd better go and get some sugar from my neighbour. So I left the house and went to my next door neighbour's home. Now this neighbour was a pig, and he wasn't real bright either. He had built his whole house of straw. Do you believe that? Who would build their house out of straw? So of course the minute I knocked on the straw house the door fell in. And do you know what? Right under that straw door was the first little pig. Dead as a door mat. He had been home the whole time.*
>
> *It seemed a shame to leave a perfectly good ham dinner lying there, so I ate it up. Think of it a big cheeseburger just waiting there to be eaten. I was feeling a little better but I still didn't have that cup of*

sugar for granny, so I went along to the next house. Now this place was the second little pig's house. He was a little brighter but not by much. He had built his home out of sticks. I rang the bell on the stick house. No answer. I called, 'Little pig, little pig, are you in?' And do you know what that rude little porker answered. 'Go away wolf you can't come in. I'm shaving the hairs on my chin chin chin.' Talk about impolite. He probably had a whole sack full of sugar and he wouldn't give me a cup for my dear old granny's birthday cake. What a pig! So I started to get a little anxious, and then I felt a sneeze coming on. Well, I huffed and I snuffed and I sneezed a great sneeze. And do you know what happened? That whole stick house fell down and right in the middle of the sticks was the second little pig, dead as a doornail.

You know that ham will spoil if it is left out in the open. So I had dinner again. Think of it as a second helping. Well, my tummy was full but I still had no sugar for dear old granny, so I went on the road again. I arrived at the third little pig's house. He must have been the brains of the family. He had built his house out of bricks. A brick house. I rang the bell on the brick house and the pig screamed through the door, 'Go away wolf, I don't want you in. Your old granny can go sit on a pin!' Well, I am usually a pretty calm fellow but when someone talks about my granny like that I go a little crazy. So of course when the cops drove up I was banging on the brick door, stomping and carrying on, making a real scene.

The rest as they say is history. I was arrested and taken down to the pigs' watch house. The newspapers were there. They figured a story about a sick wolf going to get some sugar for his dear old granny's birthday cake didn't sound all that exciting. So they jazzed up the story with all of this 'Huff and puff and blow your house down stuff.' They made me the big bad wolf. That's it. I was framed.
But maybe you could loan me a cup of sugar.

Adapted from Jon Scieszka

The teacher also wants the students to construct in this episode their own images of Alex and the pigs, and he reminds the group that only a few pictures from the book will be shown. It is important that the students begin the story in their own minds; he is concerned that the evocative pictures of the book's illustrator will lock the participants into one perspective. The teacher's telling or reading of the story has to create the evocative pictures within the students' imagination.

While the teacher knows that the humour of the story is a good release for the group and immediately arrests their interest, he also is aware that they will move significantly from their initially conventional responses. The praxis will explore notions of wolfness and it will challenge the students to commit to a conception of wolfness. The group will contemplate how stereotypes are formed and what function they serve. At the core of this pedagogical and artistic approach, then, is a teacher's wish to break down the stereotype, enable students to consider and tolerate ambiguity, and help them struggle with contradictory viewpoints of the world.

Praxis principle 1: Driven by inquiry

Strategy:
- Teacher as artful selector of material which can arouse passion.
- Teacher as storyteller able to create an imaginary world, a fictitious platform, in which important questions can be explored.

Episode 2: Defending a wolf

Once the story is completed the teacher immediately assumes the role of a reluctant defence attorney. 'I am afraid this case is going to be one of the most difficult we've faced', he suggests. 'I mean we have a confession here from Alexander, a confession that he devoured these porkers and, as we know, wolves are the natural predators of pigs.' While the teacher paces around the room and walks through the cluster of students sitting on the floor, he reminds the group of their own proficiency as lawyers and that some of them have defended the most spurious animals, such as O. J. Duck, Hannibal the Hippo and Lee Harvey Rabbit. 'You wouldn't be here if you weren't the best', he reflects. 'I wonder where we should begin?'

In role the teacher is constructing a narrative through which the students can find their voice. Gradually options are suggested. 'We could make out that his allergies were a contributing factor', ponders one participant. 'Yeah,' replies another, 'he was melancholic, like Post Melancholic Tension, a PMT defence.' The teacher supports this approach but wonders whether Alex's frightening wolfness would convince a jury. As other options are aired and debated, the lead lawyer continues to canvass what appropriate tactics might be.

While the praxis is being shaped by teacher and students, the leader knows that a pedagogical principle in these opening moments is to raise the possibilities for exploration rather than shutting them down. So the teacher challenges the credibility of a defence tactic or he invites alternative possibilities. The teacher as co-artist assumes a variety of postures, including facilitator, interrogator and manipulator as the group discovers their questions for inquiry.

Praxis principle 2: Teacher as artist (facilitator, director, interrogator, manipulator)

Strategy:
■ The teacher in role helps focus the group's attention from within the passion and builds the participants' belief in their own roles and attitudes. The teacher in role, while incorporating the skills of acting, is not an actor in the conventional sense but rather is conscious of how the role's pedagogical function can push the group to commit to the imaginary world.

Episode 3: Gathering data

The teacher in role ceases the drama praxis at the moment where the group's interest seems baited and nagging areas for investigation are revealed. They decide on how further data might be collected. Who would have information which could substantiate Alexander's version of events? Which animals or people might hold knowledge valuable to the defence? A list is made of potential sources: for example, the members of Alex's family, neighbours, the arresting officers, the medical profession.

Half the group assume the role of someone from the above list, the other half are the attorneys from Episode 2. While the lawyers contemplate what questions they will ask their eventual partners, the teacher calls the interviewees to one corner of the room. He confidentially suggests to them that they have something to hide and that they may hold damaging information which could incriminate Alexander. The interviews are then conducted.

Praxis principle 3: Promotes yearning for understanding

Strategy:
■ Students in pairs assume roles and examine their own questions.
■ The teacher places a constraint on the role-play (i.e., the interviewees have something to hide). This constraint adds a sub-text which is potentially more dramatic than role-playing scenes where no motivation for action exists.

Episode 4: Analysing and presenting data
When the interviews close, the spatial pattern of the room is transformed. The interviewers, the attorneys, sit in a circle on the floor with the teacher, while the others sit on chairs behind their partners. Those on chairs are instructed to listen to the analysis provided by the attorneys and note patterns which seem to emerge.

The attorneys report on their fieldwork and tell conflicting tales of wolf abuse, pig vendettas, and a withdrawn Alexander in childhood. To what extent can these reports be corroborated?, asks the teacher. How do you know your sources are trustworthy? The teacher consistently challenges the group on the accuracy and usefulness of their research.

Praxis principle 4: Well researched

Strategy:
- The spatial dynamic in the room is transformed to support the imaginary world.
- The teacher stage-manages the retrieval of data and reinforces with the group what material has potential for artistic endeavour.

Episode 5: Reinforcing themes
The constraint layered in Praxis principle 3, i.e. that the interviewees were hiding something, emerges in the reportback. Those listening to the data presentations commented on the contradictory facets to Alexander's life, a virtual public persona versus a private one. The teacher deliberately folded in this constraint knowing that drama praxis often is most fulfilling when contradictory themes emerge and when students have to locate themselves within those themes.

Two volunteers record the features of the public Alex and the private Alex on a chalkboard. The group's most significant data is now documented for all the attorneys to read and note. There is much discussion about what this record reveals and what value it has. The details are numerous and the possibilities endless.

Praxis principle 5: Generates rather than transmits knowledge

Strategy:
- The teacher reinforces the tension between the public image and the private face as this tension is at the core of theatreform.

Episode 6: The pigs unite
The teacher recognises that when students commit to the situation rather than the role, they will develop multiple perspectives on the one event and, then, will comprehensively consider the nature of wolfness and of stereotype. In this episode, the participants are challenged to shift their focus from the attorneys' viewpoint to that of the pigs'.

The students are asked to sit formally in horizontal rows in front of the chalkboard. The teacher suggests they examine the information on the board. What does it tell us about Alexander? What defence strategies seem strong? The students bow their heads and are told, curiously, to 'think pig'. What are the dominant images that come to mind when you 'think pig'? Some participants snort, others speak of dirt, disease, forbidden meat.

'Comrades, look at this discovery,' the teacher begins in role as the pigs' heads are raised to the chalkboard, 'what a rich opportunity we have to turn the tide on that murderous wolf and his representatives'. The pig leader points to the board and notes the various strategies of the attorneys. 'Do they honestly think they can fool us?', he asks. 'We control this town and we'll control this wolf. I won't tell you how I managed to get this information from our opponents. A spot of luck and a bit of intimidation always helps.'

The students recognise that they have changed roles and fiendishly agree with their villainous leader that they are capable of sabotaging the defence now that they have an insider's view. 'We are used to playing dirty when we have to and this may be one such occasion.' The leader reminds his comrades if the defence decides to run with a PMT defence they, the pigs, may have to counter with deliberate smear tactics. He invites them to consider ruthless means by which they could undermine Alexander's defence. 'Revealing incriminating evidence', says one. 'Throwing doubt in the jurors' minds', suggests another. The comrades are invited to think of the most scurrilous 'bit of sleaze' about Alexander. 'Make up some gossip my friends,' instructs the leader, 'and then stand up.' Slowly the individuals stand. The students are challenged to release themselves from a wolf allegiance and develop a counter-perspective on the same event.

Praxis principle 6: A tightly balanced yet flexible structure

Strategy:
- Teacher structures the work so that participants can commit to multiple perspectives on the situation, and begin to see through different eyes. Locked into one role for too long a period can limit the global perspective participants can develop.

Episode 7: Stereotypes grow

In this episode, the group play a game, 'Trading Rumours'.
Each person continually swaps their sleazy news with a partner.
As new sleaze is heard and traded, a gossip community is created.
The momentum against Alexander is growing as stereotypical
notions of wolves are securely confirmed. The students are both
the recipients and transmitters of this stereotype. In earlier episodes
they considered tactics by which the stereotype could be questioned
and now they perpetuate and embellish conventional readings of
wolfness. They control and are controlled by the medium, being both
participants and spectators in the construction and de-construction
of a common stereotype. The teacher deliberately works to create
experiences through which the participants submit to and are in
control of the storydrama. The episode closes with the students being
asked to remember the last 'bit of sleaze' they heard.

Praxis principle 7: Pursues engagement and detachment

Strategy:
- A game is played to highlight the features and themes of the work to date, and to add a scenic backdrop to the drama.

Episode 8: Betraying a wolf

The whole group sit in chairs in a large circle. The teacher waits,
stares suspiciously at certain people, and begins in an accusatory
tone as some members laugh over the recent sleaze being shared. 'I
fail to see the humour unless, of course, you have some investment
in this betrayal.' The laughter stops as the attorney stands. 'There is
a traitor among us', he continues. 'There is an evil element in this
group which has released vital tactics of ours to the pigs.' One
attorney smiles. 'If it was you,' directs the leader, 'we will find out
and you will be removed and severely punished.'

The teacher recognises that the sudden harsh tones are in sharp contrast to the mood of earlier episodes. He is taking a risk in assuming such a threatening posture but believes that the group has now sufficient knowledge where they can scrutinise their complicitous actions in the drama. 'This town is rife with the most scandalous smut about Alexander', says the leader. The attorneys are asked to share the gossip they heard. The forlorn leader walks behind them as they voluntarily voice their news. This sharing is not a humorous retelling. The teacher has deliberately managed the action where responses are seriously delivered and disturbingly contemplated. 'How are we going to rebuild Alex in the community's eyes?', ponders the leader. The group, out of role, discuss ways in which people can be rebuilt or rehabilitated within the public realm.

Praxis principle 8: Powered by risk-taking

Strategy:
■ The group is surprised when the teacher returns to the participants' original roles and challenges them on what they will do now given the opposition they face.

Episode 9: Shattering the stereotype

The students decide that the most efficient way of rebuilding Alexander would be to exploit media conventions, such as a TV Current Affairs programme or a headline in a daily paper. 'If you could have a two-minute segment in a broadcast news segment,' poses the teacher, 'what information would you convey about Alex?' The students organise themselves into small groups, they discuss and then re-create a media moment. The teacher reminds them that their broadcasts would be primarily seen by the pigs as they seem to control community life.

As the groups contemplate positive perspectives of Alex, such as his generosity, his heroism and humanity, the teacher observes how the students are now working against the wolf stereotype. They are required to reconsider a conventional understanding and then decide how their group's interpretation will be communicated within the dramatic artform. 'In a moment, pigs will be turning on their current affairs programmes,' asserts the teacher before the scenes are shared, 'and they may be surprised with what they see.' At the conclusion of each TV broadcast, the teacher asks members of the audience to comment as pig watchers might on each programme's content. For instance, one group is asked to imagine they are pig university graduates and to improvise the conversation which occurs after the broadcast. The teacher wonders to what extent the news items have provoked unsettling thoughts. Each media item confirms the wolf's rehabilitation despite the disbelief of some pigs.

The familiar media convention is an appropriate one in these concluding stages for it reveals the small group's evolving understanding and re-reading of wolfness. It enables the students to reflect in action on action. In other words, they can use the media activity to interpret and to project their view of wolfness. There is a clear logic in how the episodes have been connected. They are not randomly linked as beads on a chain but are logically interrelated to assist the students to probe further into how perceptions are generated and accounted for.

Praxis principle 9: Logically sequenced

Strategy:
- Media conventions (e.g., TV news broadcasts) can provide a useful means for the group to present their relationship to the work in a reflective manner; as well, media can provide relief from episodes where tension has been high.

Episode 10: Contrasting images of wolfness
The session is nearly over but the teacher wants to check on the students' relationship to the work, and especially how their perspectives have transformed through the praxis. Adapting an aspect of Augusto Boal's (1995) Image Theatre, the students stand in a circle and are asked to think what a pig's primary picture of a wolf might have been *prior* to the TV broadcast in Episode 9. The students face the outside rim once they have their picture. 'When I cry Wolf,' states the teacher, 'turn into the circle and assume your posture.'

Following this activity, the students select an image a pig might have *after* watching the broadcast. 'Perhaps there is no difference from the first image', asserts the teacher before the students demonstrate their second picture of wolfness. 'That similarity in itself could be revealing.' The teacher repeats the word 'wolf' and the students simultaneously turn in and demonstrate this further image. There is an outstanding contrast in this group's two images, from the grotesque and threatening to the tortured and misunderstood. The teacher highlights this contrast by orchestrating a gradual transformation from one image to the next. 'You have displayed two compelling yet different versions of the same subject', contemplates the teacher as the work concludes.

How is it possible for intelligent individuals to demonstrate such seeming opposites? How can they tolerate contradictory and ambiguous views? How do they break down stereotype and prejudice? Despite the drama's closure, the participants' artwork has begun, ironically, to question how truths are constructed and revealed in this world?

Praxis principle 10: Rich in artistry

Strategy:
- Tableau/picture theatre, while often used in the drama classroom, is a powerful means for succinctly demonstrating an attitude and position to a given topic or subject.

In summary: ten principles of drama praxis

The Alexander T. Wolf drama has taken the group on an adventure into the heart of human experience. This adventure is characterised by its collaborative quest to understand how dominant images are built, destroyed and remade. Like all valuable artistic experiences, it momentarily removes the students from their actual lives in order to get closer to them. But the artistry of the teacher is powered by an understanding of the human context. This artistry and how meanings are generated have been controlled by manipulating the three elements (people, passion and platform).

The drama demonstrates how curriculum develops in context; it is a lived and dynamic event which demands the ongoing and immediate interaction of teachers, students and their communities. The ten principles located in the Wolf drama are central to the drama praxis in this text:

1 Driven by inquiry
2 Teacher as co-artist (facilitator, director, interrogator, manipulator)
3 Promotes yearning for understanding
4 Well researched
5 Generates rather than transmits knowledge
6 Tightly balanced yet flexible structure

7 Pursues engagement and detachment

8 Powered by risk-taking

9 Logically sequenced

10 Rich in artistry

Notes

1 See Chapter 6 where I discuss Greene's work in more depth.

2 Dorothy Heathcote was appointed to the University of Durham Institute of Education (later known as Newcastle University) in 1950 at the age of 24. Her praxis revolutionised approaches to educational drama. While she has not authored a book herself, her praxis has been subjected to a comprehensive examination by B. J. Wagner (1999) in *Dorothy Heathcote: Drama as a Learning Medium* (Portland: Calender Island) and her papers assembled into an anthology by L. Johnson and C. O'Neill titled *Dorothy Heathcote: Collected Writings on Education and Drama* (London: Hutchinson, 1984). She retired in 1986. Gavin Bolton joined the staff at Durham University in 1964 and retired in 1989. With Heathcote, he analysed one of her pioneering techniques, mantle of the expert, in *Drama for Learning* (Portsmouth: Heinemann, 1995). Bolton is recognised as the one of the few educators to provide a theoretical framework through which teachers could understand drama praxis.

3 Readers are directed to the Resources section at the conclusion of this text where references by leading drama educators are listed.

References

ALBEE, E. ([1962] 1965) *Who's Afraid of Virginia Woolf?*, Harmondsworth: Penguin.

BOAL, A. (1995) *The Rainbow of Desire*, London: Routledge.

BOOTH, D. (1994) *Story Drama*, Markham, Ontario: Pembroke.

DAY, B. (1996) *This Wooden 'O': Shakespeare's Globe Reborn*, London: Oberon Books.

EISNER, E. (1991) *The Enlightened Eye: Qualitative Inquiry and the Enchantment of Educational Practice*, New York: Macmillan.

FREIRE, P. (1970) *Pedagogy of the Oppressed*, New York: Continuum.

McPHERSON, C. (1999) *The Weir and Other Plays*, New York: Theatre Communications Group.

O'BRIEN, A. and DOPIERALA, W. (1994) *The Pleasure of the Company: Drama and Teacher Education at Melbourne 1961–1994*, Melbourne: The University of Melbourne.

O'NEILL, C. (1995) *Drama Worlds: A Framework for Process Drama*, Portsmouth, N.H.: Heinemann.

SCIESZKA, J. (1989) *The True Story of the Three Little Pigs by A. Wolf* (illustrations by Lane Smith), New York: Viking Penguin.

STANISLAVSKI, C. (1949) *Building a Character*, New York, Methuen.

INTRODUCTION TO CHAPTERS 2 AND 3

In the next two chapters, I plan to focus on the drama praxis of two eminent leaders, Cecily O'Neill, an Irish-born educator who taught at the Ohio State University in the United States, and David Booth, a Canadian who lectures at the Ontario Institute for Studies in Education in Canada. Chapter 2 focuses on pre-text, a launching and weaving strategy in process drama pioneered by O'Neill. I will describe pre-text in action and illustrate its overall relationship to drama praxis. Chapter 3, examines storydrama and how it can open up the world of printed text, inform language and literacy education and help students commit to the curriculum.[1]

The following two chapters invite and challenge educators to consider the artistry of drama praxis. Although they are pitched at those beginning to learn about drama praxis, the questions raised will concern the experienced practitioner: How do these approaches fit within contemporary curriculum models? Which moments seem driven by the teacher's artistry? How are the participants drawn into the imagined world and when do they become the co-artists? What factors weaken the artistic moment?

Readers should critique the praxis presented and consider the characteristics of artistic endeavour so fundamental to its execution.

1 Readers are referred to my monograph *Pretext and Storydrama: The Artistry of Cecily O'Neill and David Booth* (Brisbane: NADIE Publications, 1995).

While the praxis described has been developed by leaders in the field, it would be misleading to claim that the work was not contentious in parts. This statement will not surprise the experienced theatregoer who can never guarantee that a theatre event will always bring a satisfactory response; the work is powered by a group dynamic composed of various cultural, sexual, gendered and physiological identities. I have alerted readers to those moments in the drama praxis where a seeming dissatisfaction surfaced. Chapter 3 concludes with my adaptation of the major features of the artistry discussed to the general school curriculum.

Chapter 2 — Getting started with good pre-texts

Pre-text

❝ *My purpose was to develop an extended piece of practical work in drama at the participants' own level, in order to provide material for reflection on the nature of the process. I was also interested in investigating the way in which the pre-text, in this case a folk tale, defines the world of the drama and engenders the emerging themes in the work.*

I believe that process drama can be a significant vehicle for prolonged and satisfying experimental encounters with the dramatic medium. Although the extended and essentially improvisatory event that is beginning to be known as process drama will proceed without a pre-written script, an original text is generated in action. The resulting experience for the participants can possess the same coherence, complexity and singularity of any satisfying event. Process drama, while remaining apparently formless and undefined by a previous plan or script has a special capacity to lay bare the basic dramatic structures that give it life, which it shares with other kinds of theatre.

(Cecily O'Neill[1])

Background and key terms

Thirty-five leading educators in drama praxis assemble to participate in an extended process drama over two days. For many, this will be the first time that they have experienced, as a student, an improvised drama since their undergraduate years; their professional lives now are ruled by their ability to lead and not participate.

O'Neill and the group seem to share a common understanding. They know, for instance, that it would be unlikely that the two days would conclude with a public performance of their work. This workshop is not for actors and the refining of their performance skills. It is pitched at drama leaders wanting to probe further into what makes for sound improvisation and how they, as teachers and arts practitioners, can become more adept at structuring improvisation. They recognise the power of negotiated drama as a vehicle for helping children articulate their own special relationship to the world. The terms 'process drama' and 'pre-text' are ones O'Neill finds useful when characterising the nature and launching strategy, respectively, of non-scripted collaborative enactment.[2] The participants are familiar with O'Neill's work and accept the working definitions which follow.

The features of process drama include:
- Separate scenic units linked in an organic manner
- Thematic exploration rather than an isolated or random skit or sketch
- A happening and an experience which does not depend on a written script
- A concern with participants' change in outlook
- Improvisational activity
- Outcomes not predetermined but discovered in process
- A script generated through action
- The leader actively working both within and outside the drama

---

Fundamental to O'Neill's understanding of process drama is the central role the teacher plays in weaving the artistic event. Rather than a passive observer of the child's drama, O'Neill is proactive in structuring the work. This proactivity does not simply mean that the teacher instructs the group what to do, but rather negotiates and renegotiates the substance and direction of the drama towards an aesthetic experience.

Teachers in process drama should see themselves as:
- Structure operators who weave the units of action together into an artful experience
- Artists, the teachers, collaborating with their students, the co-artists
- Building a work in process
- Able to release themselves from their lesson plan
- Capable of finding questions to explore than answers to provide
- Raising possibilities rather than confirming probabilities

The launching strategy in process drama is fundamental to its development. O'Neill calls this launching strategy a pre-text.

A pre-text:
- Rings up the curtain by framing the participants effectively and economically in roles that have a firm association with the potential action
- Suggests clear purposes and tasks
- Structural function may be to set up expectations, establish patterns, imply roles, suggest a setting
- Operates as an animating current
- Sets in motion the weaving of the drama: a text is generated by this process
- Hints at previous events and foreshadows future occurrences
- Can be recalled or repeated
- Is not necessarily a text to be written down
- Will give birth to any number of themes

O'Neill finds it useful to consider how playwrights use dramatic form when devising opening scenes. Shakespeare, for instance, usually has the first scene contain the seeds of the forthcoming action. In *Macbeth*, the three witches neatly set in motion the action of the play by introducing darkness/lightness, winning/losing, right/wrong. *Hamlet*, likewise, introduces the themes of deception, disarray and superstition in the beginning minutes. Our attention is arrested usually by the detail which is not provided: questions are raised, possibilities considered, a future suggested. Drama teachers, equally, should look for similar portents or echoes of foreboding when they devise their pre-text. A photograph may be an effective pre-text, a gesture, a title, a location, an object or an image, or a classic text which is reborn through the drama.

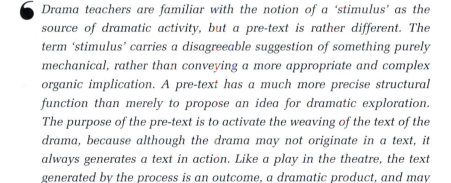

Drama teachers are familiar with the notion of a 'stimulus' as the source of dramatic activity, but a pre-text is rather different. The term 'stimulus' carries a disagreeable suggestion of something purely mechanical, rather than conveying a more appropriate and complex organic implication. A pre-text has a much more precise structural function than merely to propose an idea for dramatic exploration. The purpose of the pre-text is to activate the weaving of the text of the drama, because although the drama may not originate in a text, it always generates a text in action. Like a play in the theatre, the text generated by the process is an outcome, a dramatic product, and may be recalled and to some extent repeated. (Cecily O'Neill)

Often drama teachers commence their lesson with a 'warm-up' or 'ice-breaker'. Such might involve a physical activity, perhaps a game or movement piece which would not necessarily have any relationship to the activities which followed. A pre-text, on the other hand, contains the germ of action. Within the pre-text there lies the possibilities of pursuing any particular course in the drama. It is not an isolated activity but an integral one:

> An example of an effective pre-text in process drama was the task required of a class of ten-year-olds, which arose after a class reading of the picture book Mufaro's Beautiful Daughters.[3] The work was in no way a re-enactment of the story, but confronted some of the same issues. The students were in role as advisers to a great King, who asked them to select a bride for him. During the two hour process drama that ensued, the students established criteria for selection, disguised their identities and went under cover, devised tests, answered riddles, and solved problems. They dealt with questions of gender expectations, power structures, the deception of appearances, the priorities of government, and all of these concerns were raised by the pre-text, the original task asked of the participants.
>
> This task, the pre-text, established power relations – the King, his advisers and the potential brides; it was a clear task and proposed action – the selection of a bride; it hinted at background and raised expectations among the participants. In other words, it operated not merely as a stimulus, but structurally within the process.   (Cecily O'Neill)

Pre-text and process drama

What follows now is a comprehensive description and analysis of a process drama led by O'Neill. Contained within this analysis are the words of the participants, O'Neill's observations, reflections of other theorists, and my own linking commentary. There are any number of ways in which this process drama could be analysed. The box below lists O'Neill's suggestion, which readers might adopt when organising their responses to process drama.

When analysing process drama the following organising themes or categories may be useful:
The pre-text and how it articulates with the dramatic action
Episodes or scenic units and the organic links between them
Notions of participation and audience
Engagement (suspending disbelief) and detachment (suspending belief)

> Dramatic irony
> Private and public dimensions
> Particulars and universals
> Emergent themes
> Archetypal elements
> Overlapping worlds – i.e. world of pre-text, of the drama, of the participants

In this chapter, it is the first category, i.e. how the pre-text relates to process drama and aspects of the work's artistry, which will be a focus. Readers might later consider the work through other categories listed above or, alternatively, create their own.

Episode 1: Launching the pre-text

Task: Teacher narrates the Irish folk-tale, 'The Seal Wife'.

 Long ago there lived a young fisherman named Patrick
One day he was walking by the seashore when he saw the most beautiful woman he had ever seen sitting on a rock, combing her hair
He crept up to watch her, as he did
She picked up a garment, drew it around her body and dived into the sea
She had become a seal
He walked there again the next night and again she combed her hair and covered herself in the garment and dived into the ocean
He went back again the next night and this time he seized her skin
She was completely powerless and had to follow him
She became his wife, they spent several years together and she bore three children
In a small cottage there are not many places to hide things, so he hid her skin in the thatching in the roof
As we all know thatching needs to be replaced every seven years
The thatcher was working on the roof and threw down the old thatching and with it her skin
The children found the skin, picked it up and took it to her to ask what it was
That night as the husband and children were sleeping she took the skin and fled to the sea and never came back again

The participants sit on the floor while O'Neill, seated on a stool, tells this Irish tale. The tale is characterised by its brevity and lack of illuminating detail. This pre-text anticipates numerous questions:

Why did Patrick seize the woman's skin?
What was the relationship between the woman and her family over the seven years?
How did the family cope after the woman fled to the sea?
What did the children think of their mother when she was with them and when she left them?
What does this tale teach about relationships?, about love?, about commitment?

The rich resonances of the tale with other artistic works, e.g. films like *The Piano*, *The Color Purple* and *The French Lieutenant's Woman*, and plays like, *A Streetcar Named Desire*, *The Winter's Tale* and *The Wild Duck* draw the participants into the emerging drama.

O'Neill's drama praxis is characterised by **an ability to select a pre-text which contains the seeds of inquiry**. *The Irish folk-tale raises issues related to families, identity and sacrifice which have dominated the yearnings of humans over time.*

Episode 2: Transforming the pre-text

Task: The small groups create one moment, an image, from the seven years Patrick and the seal-woman were together.

As the groups work to construct an image or tableau which satisfies all members, O'Neill notes the themes which are emerging for this group. In this context, there is a strong recurring image of child-birth and on the constant painful drawing of the seal-woman to the sea. This dominant theme later becomes a focus.

As the tableaux are shared, O'Neill is concerned with helping the spectators raise questions which will open inquiry. 'It's not always wise to prioritise the narrative,' she suggests, 'because this fixation on the linear sequence stops the meaning from resonating.'

The tableau strategy, she reminds the group, is one of the most economical ways of revealing children's relationship to the work. Tableaux challenge the participants to watch and respond. Tableaux can help students struggle with ambiguity and deal with multi-faceted readings.

The participants agree with O'Neill when she explains that a frustrating thing for students can be to deal with contradictions. 'How do we help students accept different interpretations of the same event? How can we assist students to tolerate and celebrate difference?'

She deliberately chooses a strategy, in this instance the tableau, which will force divergent thinking.

O'Neill's praxis is governed by raising possibilities rather than confirming probabilities.

It is not always possible merely to accept and use the pre-text as it stands. Any complex or elaborate pre-text, for example a myth, story or classic text, must be transformed or re-born in the drama. However, powerful traces of the original will resonate in the patterns and relationships that develop during the process. Significant dramatic experiences will not necessarily arise from simply adapting and dramatising what appear to be appropriate pre-texts. This approach is likely to lead to work that is explanatory rather than exploratory, where the ideas and themes are demonstrated and displayed rather than being discovered and explored. Ideally, the pre-text will be sufficiently distorted or reworked so as to be in effect made afresh or transformed.

(Cecily O'Neill)

Peter Abbs reminds us that in the first phase of the art-making process there is the release of an impulse, an animation towards form, or, a compulsion to symbolise.[4] In many respects, the telling of the tale in Episode 1 provides this catalyst for symbolisation. But in process drama it is the move towards physicalising that impulse which triggers the participants to shape their private image into public display. The tableau is an ideal ploy in this initial stage of playmaking. It does not commit the participants to a particular interpretation but rather offers the possibility of multiple interpretations.

Episode 3: Three creations from the tableaux

Task: In turn, those representing the seal-wives, the Patricks, and the children are removed from the tableaux and lined up for contemplation.

O'Neill challenges the participants to look closely at the representations which the small groups have constructed. She seeks a range of strategies through which the spectators can be supported in their looking. At times, she provides her own observations, at other times the spectators voice how the image appears to them.

When the children are finally lined up neither O'Neill nor the group seem satisfied with this bland display. 'Let's change this slightly,' she says, 'let's bring in the mother whose hair was being pulled in one of the tableau, the mother with the babe in her arms.' The children now randomly express their thoughts as the mother stands amongst them.

The teacher structures a moment which supports the experience of those who display and those who watch the display. Again, there is an emphasis in **helping people attend to the moment so that it can be re-born and will fertilise within them***.*

A feature of this way of working is the demand placed on participants to articulate what it is they see and to be never completely satisfied with the certainty of their observation. In this respect, O'Neill echoes the concerns of the eminent American arts philosopher, Maxine Greene. It is never enough to attend to an artwork as something out there that has been defined by official others to be perceived, read, or heard as those others decide. The works at hand, Greene contemplates, should become 'objects of experience' for those who come to them:

> *Such requires an energy, a reaching out, and a care, even a solicitude in noticing, in paying heed to nuance and to detail, and then ordering the parts perceived into a whole within experience.*[5]

'We as teachers are obligated to enable our students to attend well, to pay heed, to notice what might not be noticed in a careless reading or inattentive watching', says Greene. Spaces need to be created for students' meaning-making, for their interpretations and struggles, which are bound to be numerous.[6] In process drama strategies are structured which facilitate and empower students to attend to the work and create multiple meanings.

Episode 4: Becoming a community

Entering into the community of the fisherman and seal-woman occurs through two tasks:

Task 1: 'You are now marked off by your attitude to the seal wife', O'Neill suggests to the whole group. 'Share your attitudes, thoughts, rumours, something you heard, something you saw, or perhaps even something you made up.'

Task 2: Each participant selects a word or phrase from their trading above. Those words are repeated frenetically as participants move around the space. As the group whisper secretively to one another, O'Neill orchestrates their whisperings so that voices rise and fall in a chorus of suspicion and alienation.

O'Neill likens this strategy to 'brushing in a background'. The details are still thin and the emphasis is on simplicity. A narrative has begun to form, a narrative which evolves from the participants' own reading of the events. 'Simplify and be non-specific', O'Neill reminds the group. 'The folktale is by nature non-specific.'

One participant was struck by the organic nature of structure. 'This work is growing, evolving and being shaped by the participants' existing knowledge and experiences, and that knowledge which we create in the here and now.'[7]

> *The teacher's drama praxis is tied into developing a sense of community, a community which both controls and is controlled by the form.*

Greene reminds us that community cannot be produced through rational formulation or by edict. Like freedom, it has to be 'achieved by persons offered a space in which to discover what they recognise together' and appreciate in common. Wright concurs, 'What unites us is the common experience, the investment of time and energy and our innate desire to "story", that is, to make sense of our experience.'[8]

Episode 5: The family

Task 1: The group is divided into pairs; one assumes the role of the seal-woman, the other the role of her child. The children sit on the floor with O'Neill; the partners remain an audience.

Task 2: O'Neill assumes the role of the newly arrived schoolteacher. She explains that there is a new project which the class will work on: the sea. 'What do you know about the sea?' 'Shells', says one. 'Fish and water', says another. And then, seemingly uncomfortable with the implication of the subject, one child asks, 'Do we have to do the sea topic?' 'I'm sure', retorts the teacher, 'you'll find some aspect of it that you'll find interesting.'

Task 3: The children return to their parent and ask for information about the sea.

Task 4: At the school, the children retell what their mothers have told them about the sea, but not naturalistically, more as a collage of voices, speaking as and when they wish.

The participants now move from playing the roles of the wider community members who have developed certain attitudes to the seal-woman and her family, to enact members of the family itself. Artistry here is concerned with not locking the participants into one role for too long. O'Neill is suspicious of the kind of drama teaching which demands that students project themselves into the life of a character for a sustained period of time. She is interested in having participants 'project into the situation in its entirety'. This projection requires participants having access to multiple roles and viewpoints.

O'Neill's attention is arrested by the dramatic action, and the behaviours that people adopt within that action, and the consequent responsibilities and demands which then ensue. Distance from the work is important to developing such projection: 'Engagement in process drama offers participants the opportunity to explore and realise a range of values and identities and experiment with alternate versions of humanity.' She wants students to develop their own reading of an event which could be compounded if an individual is trapped into one role for any period of time. This accounts for the non-naturalistic reporting of what the children discovered in Task 4.

O'Neill deliberately focuses on the seal-woman in the pair activity for this woman had emerged as a key theme in the participants' tableaux.

As the children in Task 3 returned to their 'mother', O'Neill interjected, concerned with the level of noise, 'The volume in the room is very important. There is too much noise here. Let's gear it down.' The leader, like the participants, has an investment in the drama's evolution and deliberately shapes a construct in which projection occurs. When later challenged on this interjection, O'Neill responded, 'I consciously took this risk in order to give people space.'

In recognition that the mother/child pairs had built up a close bonding O'Neill suggests that each pair spends time debriefing. As one participant later recalled:

It was valuable to feel what it is like to be in a student-role again and to recognise how necessary and important is a leader's sensitivity to group dynamics. There were times when issues and feelings were potentially threatening to emotional equilibrium and it was necessary to feel that the group leader was dependable and aware.[9]

Leaders' responses and decision-making in similar episodes have been subjected to considerable criticism from sceptics of process drama: What function does the teacher have? When should teachers assert their own reading of a classroom event? To what extent should teachers layer into the work their own expectations? How do teachers know which risks to take?

A feature of O'Neill's artistry is that she not only construes herself as a co-conspirator with the students but also is sensitive to her own role as leader of an educational experience. Like a painter she manipulates the canvas with her brush, introducing elements which may not have been predicted. The evolving piece gradually suggests possibilities to the artist. At the same time, these possibilities are informed by O'Neill's understanding of what process drama is and what it is not. She knows, for example, that she is not training actors for an academy, i.e. students are not building skills of characterisation for theatrical performance.

Her drama praxis does not culminate in one aesthetic product which can be assessed and applauded but is driven by an aesthetic process with numerous products to be scrutinised for what they teach. 'It is the responsibility of the teacher or leader', she says, 'to find a focus that creates an imperative tension and provides a vehicle for the themes and images to be explored.'

O'Neill's weaving of the units of action led to one observer's reflection:

> *The tension of being both in role as an individual and at the same time in a composite role because we were all seal-wives and all children is something I have used but not in such a formal setting. Having*

the mothers sit behind the children was important; not being able to look at 'my' mother's face to gauge her reaction I was not sure how to react and this added a further tension and made the connection with my mother stronger . . . I wonder how much of my own life experiences which were brought to the surface contribute to my feelings of significance?[10]

The artist releases the participants from the burden of characterisation and presses into the work multiple role perspectives.

Episode 6: The Private Dreamworld

Task 1: The group is divided into two; one group will enact the fisherman's dream while the other will enact the seal-woman's.

Task 2: Each participant writes a song, prayer, letter, prophesy, indictment or poem, from the perspective of the fisherman, the seal-woman, the children, or someone else in the community.

Task 3: After a break, the feeling level of the work is re-established through a game. In pairs, each partner, eyes shut, gets to know the other's hands. Then they separate, and move about, still blind, trying to identify their partner's hands from among all the people in the group.

Dreams are a useful vehicle for tapping into the private world of a character. Dreams are never naturalistic. This fact releases the participants to use sounds, movement, music, and words in an abstract fashion. Dreams are also profoundly theatrical and O'Neill reminds the group of how Shakespeare employs them in *Julius Caesar*, *Richard III* and *A Midsummer Night's Dream*.

The half-groups are large and the participants experience difficulty in arriving at a decision. O'Neill challenges the fisherman's group to consider Patrick's emotional state. The net becomes a powerful symbol for this group. They experiment with throwing it out and heaving it in. The dreamer, Patrick, is ultimately drawn into the net with the seal-woman.

The other group's dream of the seal-woman consists of a multitude of images. One audience member, after watching it, described it by listing her recurring observations, 'Moaning, clapping, people hanging off the wall, turmoil of the sea, grabbing, reaching, marriage bed, ocean rolling in to the shore, a couple with arms around each other, ongoing moaning, frightened sounds, SCREAMING, running, stop.'[11]

Another perceived it as a more truthful account of this woman's life, 'The dream content necessitated going into the seal-wife's head as opposed to representing outward social relations, the consequence of which was the creation of images of the character as individual, many of which were divorced from her role as wife and mother.'[12]

The writing which followed confirmed a focus on the seal-woman's angst:

> *leave me…let me*
> *go…my feet are*

> *torn and bleeding…*
> *I need to float*
> *in freedom*
>
> *Beauty and mystery spiralling in ever circles of*
> *Laughter joy and be giggling playful delight*
> *'Til pull back strange; cannot move entrapped*
> *Heart fights, mind alert, body obedient to*
> *Giving birth after rape after birth after rape…*
>
> The hand-finding activity allowed the participants to recapture that tension and confirm the themes which were emerging from the drama, themes related to family ties, bonding, responsibility and loss. 'It's a game of searching and rejection', said O'Neill. In this respect, the game is a dynamic illuminator of the human condition which has been echoing through the work. Unfortunately, most teachers misunderstand how games should be used in drama classes and tend to exploit them as ice-breakers only.

The juxtaposition of the public world with the private one is a feature of O'Neill's artistic practice. In Episode 5, the children had public demands placed on them to perform a duty, i.e. school work, but these demands were compromised in light of the private conversations with their parent. Drama operates on this tension between the presentation and realisation of self.

Shakespeare's plays richly capture this tension. In *Macbeth*, for example, Lady Macbeth summons up the spirits of evil to represent the incarnation of the devil as she carries out King Duncan's assassination. 'Look like the innocent flower,' she cries to her husband on the eve of the murder, 'but be the serpent underneath.' When Duncan arrives at their home with the words 'This castle hath a pleasant seat; the air / Nimbly and sweetly recommends itself / Unto our gentle senses', he says one of the classic lines of dramatic irony. Process drama, O'Neill believes, can exploit equally these tensions between public expectation and private knowing.

> **Drama praxis is informed by a rich understanding of the artform.**

Episode 7: Adapting the forum theatre

The next phase of the work moves the action beyond the framework of the story. 'Ten years have passed, narrates the leader, since the Seal Wife returned to the sea.'

Task 1: O'Neill questions the group on the circumstances which might lead to the children wanting to know more about their mother from the fisherman.

Task 2: A reworked forum theatre strategy is employed where two participants enact the roles of the fisherman and his sixteen-year-old daughter. The group decides on the setting (a rock by the seashore), and the circumstance (the eldest daughter is in love and seeks advice from her father). The spectators suggest the dialogue and staging which occurs.

Task 3: Dividing into groups of six, each participant writes one line of the dialogue between father and daughter. This contribution is a private one which no other member has access to. A random text is created.

Task 4: Groups exchange their six-line scripts and then stage the scene they have received between father and daughter.

Despite the fact that roles are cast in the second task, it is evident that all participants have a stake in the action. In previous steps they have committed themselves to both the family and the community and are therefore involved in honouring the scene which is now to be played between the fisherman and his daughter. Reworking Augusto Boal's forum theatre technique,[13] O'Neill solicits advice from the audience on what the major themes would be as father and daughter engage in this moment. 'Whose space is it?', she asks when deciding on the location. 'Who will speak first?' The spectators playwright the scene and seem conscious of their own skill as dramatists actively shaping dramatic form.

The participant who plays Patrick peers out to the sea, the daughter, named Katrina by the group enters. One member of the audience calls out, 'It's dusk,' before Patrick speaks:

PATRICK: *You look as though you have news.*

KATRINA: [Looking uncomfortable and nervous. Moving from foot to foot, smiling.] *I just had to come here. It's so lovely.*

PATRICK: *Are you in love?*

KATRINA: [giggles] *I don't know. Dad, talk to me.*

PATRICK: *About what?*

KATRINA: *About mum and you, and what it was like – just what you want to say.*

PATRICK: *What do you want to know?*

KATRINA: *The others are asleep now – there is time to talk to me.*

PATRICK: *I loved your mother more than anything. She was the most beautiful woman I had ever seen.*

O'Neill cuts through the dialogue and asks the group, 'What do we have so far?' Ideas flood from the participants.
'Fantastic tension', says one.
'He says everything before she does', calls out another.
'It's not what she wants to say!'
'She doesn't know what she wants to know.'

'He knows that she needs to know.'
'He says things before she does to block the opportunity for her to say them.'

O'Neill listens to all these responses, nodding and agreeing.
'I wonder', she muses, 'what the daughter can ask that Patrick can't squirm out of?'
'How did you meet my mother?', suggests one.
Recognising how difficult the task might be for the two actors, and concerned that the spectators are now settling down as audience, O'Neill replies, 'Oh, it's not fair to ask these two to do this.'

The previous work has prepared the participants to think of themselves as artists shaping content and form. The tableaux activity (Episodes 2 and 3) and the dream re-enactment (Episode 6) focused on helping the group attend to the created moment. O'Neill often incorporates forum theatre into process drama because the spectators (or spect-actors)[14] have an investment in the product's evolution. 'The encounter is being monitored', she claims, 'and structured by the observers, who, because of their previous involvement, have a considerable investment in it.'

The forum theatre is not played through to a culminating point. 'It's about stopping at the moment before it begins to get weaker,' she asserts, 'before it gets to be less.' Process drama, she repeats, is partly about participants developing the skills to become spectators to their own work and thereby capable of exercising control over it.

The whole group takes on the responsibility of the performers in Task 3 by creating their own scripted text, but it is a fragmented text. 'I rejected the idea of dividing the group into all fathers and daughters', she later explains. 'I am in the business of dislocating young minds and am keenly searching for strategies which unsettle, create ambiguity, and force students to struggle with contradictions.' The random text activity, and its staging by the small groups, challenges the participants to work simultaneously as technicians and playwrights by directing a potentially senseless piece with clarity and meaning.

Works of art live through the active engagement and detachment of the viewer with the object. **Fundamental to O'Neill's praxis is the deliberate selection of strategies that pursue engagement and detachment.**

Often satisfying encounters with artistic works are controlled by a viewer's investment in remaining with the piece, an uncompromising desire to be satisfied, and a belief in value and achievement. In this seventh phase of the drama structure, we can see the leader's quest to develop in her students this sense of control and accomplishment in what is created. Through the process drama, the participants are refining their artistic skills to judge the aptness of a phrase or gesture, to assess the locale and staging, to probe what surprises and what opens up indefinable possibilities.

Critics of this mode of working, which has crudely and naively been referred to as 'a learning medium', misjudge the artistic skills that both leaders and their students are clearly cultivating.[15] As one participant reflected, 'O'Neill is a performance artist who manipulates the drama with the perceptions and skills normally associated with contemporary directors of distinction.' Recalling the manner in which she weaved an aesthetic tapestry which would release the participants to venture into their own association with the pre-text, this participant elaborated:

> *Her acknowledgment that the drama teacher is an artist with an agenda precluded the impression, given by so many weak exponents of the art, that the classroom work is somehow no more than a laissez-faire collection of random games and activities. Through O'Neill's structures we were enmeshed in a drama net via systematic use of language and action which invited us to engage, respond actively, and oppose or transform enactments . . . Her conscious linking of activities to domains as diverse as classical dramatic literature, poetry, folk saga, music, painting, music-theatre and film, indicated that process drama can also illuminate drama as an art-form, an art which presents, represents and reinterprets our social, historical and spiritual consciousness within wider aesthetic spheres.[16]*

To claim, as some have, that process drama denies an interest in artistic products and aesthetic understandings, fails to account for the dynamic interplay between participant and spectator, player and audience, watcher and watched, and creator and created: a dialogic relationship which is generated by an unquenchable thirst for understanding; a thirst and venture which is at the centre of all artistic endeavour.

Episode 8: A universe of other texts

Task 1: The groups from the previous episode randomly select one person's poem, letter or message from Episode 6, Task 2. A choral reading exercise ensues with each member of the group voicing a word, phrase or sentence from the writing in orchestrated fashion.

Task 2: Three new groups are told that the story is now a thousand years on. 'A trace of the original story', O'Neill asserts, 'now exists in a folk dance.' The groups each create a simple folk dance based on the legend of the seal-woman. The folk dances are shared at the Annual Anthropology Conference.

O'Neill reminds the participants that a number of texts have been generated through the process drama: the author's text, the individual's text, the director's text, the actor's text, the rehearsal text, and the audience's text are just some of these. 'Every text', she recalls, 'lives in a universe of other texts.'

Reminding the group of their pedagogical as well as their artistic function, she suggests that it is important that the children we teach have their own text honoured. 'Kids can be keen on their work but not on other's.' The first task challenges the groups to select words from the writing which have powerful resonances of the themes explored. 'Only select the words', O'Neill asserts, 'that are earning their keep and which convey strong images.' The members of each group stand in choral tradition and create a spontaneous poem.

'I don't know where Katrina's story ends', claims O'Neill when the choral poem is completed. 'The next phase might be, "I believe that in a district nearby there remains a family whose feet are webbed", or, "A proclamation now exists that you are forbidden to be in contact with anyone descended from the seal wife."' A silence ensues. O'Neill seems to change track, perhaps uncertain whether the group are willing to pursue Katrina's future.

The folk dance becomes a reflective activity where the group can reflect both in and on action. 'The dance took us 1,000 years on,' claimed one participant, 'distanced from the narrative and its immediate emotional heart.'[17] However, while the dances bring considerable release and joviality, as their titles 'Flipper', 'Sealed with a Kiss' and 'Stolen Wife' suggested, the light-hearted banter has the potential to undermine the scope and thematic import of the pre-text.

The artist searches for a dramatic form which enables the participants to reveal their relationship to the event.

Episode 9: An unsettling consummation

Task 1: The leader asks that those who can most identify with Patrick, the fisherman, move to the centre of the room.

Task 2: The remainder are the voices in Patrick's head. 'Voices,' states O'Neill, 'say the strongest thing you can to Patrick.' The Patricks keep their eyes closed and respond to the voices that circulate around them.

Task 3: The fishermen are removed to another part of the room. While they talk among themselves. O'Neill assumes the role as the head of a clinic. 'Colleagues,' she states to the others while pointing at the fishermen, 'look in your dossiers and let me know if you have come across a more dysfunctional group than these fishermen.'

Task 4: The group resist the clinician role in Task 3. Discussion occurs about the seal-woman and particularly the name she is given, 'the seal wife'. What happens to the seal-woman once she has returned to the sea? The group assume the role of the sea community and sit in a circle on the floor. 'Our sister', O'Neill asserts, 'has returned to us. Should we take her in?'

Task 5: The group jointly narrate a possible ending to the story.

Task 6: Seamus Heaney's poem, 'Maighdean Mara' ('The Sea Maiden') is given to the three groups from Episode 8, Task 2. Each group stages a choral reading of one stanza from the poem.

Recognising that the folk-dance in this context could not bring a culminating fulfilment, O'Neill asks, 'Does anyone feel more strongly mother? child? father? a member of the land or sea communities?' Someone in the group mentions Patrick's name. 'Is there any reconciliation for Patrick the fishermen?', asks O'Neill.
'He will have to find it himself', says one. 'He won't find it in the community.'
'He may wander like Oedipus', posits another.

When the voices assault the all-male Patricks in Task 2, O'Neill allows the men to speak to the whole group. In turn they reflect:
'It's easy to know when it's too late.'
'Let he who is without sin cast the first stone.'
'I knew it was wrong.'
'Confused messages.'
'Accusations.'

The men playing Patrick seem in despair and emotionally exhausted by the activity, a contrasting atmosphere from the folk-dance. Some members of the group confirm this observation and wonder whether it is fair that such power was given to the voices. 'They are not embodying Patrick', defends O'Neill. 'We are creating contrary points of view that do not always have to be sugar-coated.' Pressing the group further on the nature of artistic experience, 'At a particular level there is nothing more useless than compassion.'

O'Neill, in Task 4, provides a further example of how the group might explore the phenomenon of Patrick, but this invitation is resisted. 'We are no longer in the myth', asserts one participant. 'It makes it too specific.' As the group debates this strategy, one voice cuts through the discussion, 'What about the lack of identity of the seal-wife? Why is she given this title, wife, anyway?'
'Her identity is taken from her,' muses O'Neill, 'and then seven years later she reclaims it.'
Contemplating a way of closure, one participant asks, 'What about the legend as told by the seals?'
'Another possible way', interjects another, 'would be to see what happens when the seal-wife goes back home.'
The participants now consider what her life was like in the sea. There is much interest in this idea.
'Now we're cooking with gas!' O'Neill retorts, noting the possibility for the participants to explore their own journey and interaction with the pre-text.

The final tasks bring closure to the drama by recalling and reminding the group of the journey which inspired their drama and which informed the pre-text.

Artistry in process drama releases the leader from the burden of planning and invites the participants to co-create the text based on their own desires, needs and agendas.

As the group enact the gathering of the seals who must decide whether their sister, the seal-woman, should be rehabilitated to the group, a theme emerges, one of ownership and rejection. 'Our sister', O'Neill states, 'has returned to us – should we take her in? Is she still one of us?' The seals seem unwilling to accept her. 'She will have strange ways', claims one. 'She has been defiled', asserts another. A seemingly lone voice rebukes the group for alienating their sister, and demands that they see her as having an identity beyond that of mother and wife. In response, one male participant asks, 'What bull among you would take her?' 'TAKE HER!!!', repeat some members of the group in astonishment.

For one participant the direction of this meeting was painful and brought a challenging rebuke:

 This exercise came immediately on top of the discussion of the name Seal Wife and was perceived by several of the group (myself included) as an opportunity for the character to be taken out of the context of wife and mother and reinstated with her own self identity. As it turned out, the results were not as I anticipated for the majority of the group refused to accept her on the grounds that 1. she had deserted her children 2. she had deserted her husband 3. she was polluted by her association with humans and 4. her own vanity had been the cause of what was then a deserved fate. In all of these responses she is marginalised, the other and the lesser of her children, her husband, her society and her rapist. The responses came from a range of sub-ject positions with many of them indicators of the personal agenda of the respondents or reflections of societal thinking.

Personally I found the responses enormously disturbing and at one point was on the verge of leaving the room. My interjections were designed to 'make' the others recognise that the female victims of society are so often doubly victimised. Firstly they are raped and then held personally responsible for the assault or post rape and they are shunned by society as soiled. Furthermore, as a victim of Patrick's (masculinist) quest for ownership of property – in this case the seal woman – she then became a tool for the valuing of phallocentric moral codes which dictate the woman as subservient to her family. The activity provided an ideal platform for the interrogation of value systems constructed to appear natural, universal and objective. I was disappointed that this opportunity was missed . . .[18]

This response appears more directed at the viewpoints expressed by the group and the leader's reluctance to assume a feminist agenda, an agenda as characterised by the above author. This view was not shared by other participants. 'If you always see the world through one perspective', argued Rob Galbraith, 'you are unable to participate in a learning experience through experiencing another perspective.' A pursuit of political correctness, this author suggested, predetermines the outcome, passes moral judgements on participants' responses in role play, and inevitably inhibits students to discover the truth for themselves. 'Surely the real truth, pathos, sadness, tragedy, implications of the story of the seal wife', concludes Galbraith, 'might best be shown through the perspective of the bull seals who refuse to take her back?'[19]

At the core of artistic practice, argues Maxine Greene, are the elements of reflectiveness, self-discovery and surprise. Aesthetic works open up diverse ways of being, and of knowing and of art-making. There is a 'forever unfinished dialogue' provoked by works of art 'in their wonderful incompleteness'. It seems to me that to conclude a drama with a recognised platitude, a moral certainty or a political correctness denies the vision and possibility to which artistic works aspire. The bottom line is that participants create their own response to the work based on their particular educational, cultural and ethical context. 'Again it is a matter of awakening imaginative capacities', Greene proposes, 'and of appealing to people's freedom.'[20]

Free human beings can choose, can move beyond where they are, can ascend to places of which, in their ordinariness, they could have had no idea, and it is **to these powers of imagination which artistry can claim**.

Conclusion

This drama praxis highlights the ambiguous roles of the leader and participants, roles which are multi-faceted and require the capacity to control, submit, direct, and collaborate. Teachers have to find a delicate balance between their own intentions in the drama and those of their students. In other words, 'to lead the way', as O'Neill says, 'while walking backwards'. Leaders, she argues, will need to act as guides who should 'know where the travellers have come from, and the nature of journey so far, as to help to determine the kind of journey which lies ahead'.

Throughout this chapter, readers will have noted how the contextual circumstances impact upon the development of the work. Process drama is driven by group effort. The participants' experiences captured within this example of drama praxis inevitably will be different from others' experience at different places with the same pre-text. This reason is one for including the participants' words, wherever possible, so that readers can be provided with a feel for the data which emerged from this context.

Readers will note how O'Neill responded to these contextual circumstances, especially in the latter episodes, and revisited her plan in the immediate circumstances. Her praxis is driven, it seems to me, by this rare capacity to empathise with the participants and to take risks in process. As a result, participants believe themselves to be more in control of the work and responsible for its consummation. In process drama, then, one of the primary outcomes of the journey is the consummated experience of the journey itself:

> *Working from a powerful pre-text, we can harness students' imaginations, create dramatic contexts for learning, provide complex language opportunities and furnish them with significant dramatic experience. With an understanding of dramatic tension and structure, it will be possible to achieve the same dynamic organisations that gives form to theatre experience. We must recognise that process drama is a significant dramatic mode, springing from the same dramatic roots and obeying the same dynamic rules that shape the development of any effective theatre event.* (Cecily O'Neill)

Notes

1 Unless otherwise stated, all O'Neill references in this chapter are contained within my monograph, *Pretext and Storydrama* (Brisbane: NADIE Publications, 1995).
2 See John O'Toole, *The Process of Drama* (London: Routledge, 1992); Dorothy Heathcote and Gavin Bolton, *Drama for Learning* (Portsmouth, N.H.: Heinemann, 1995); Michael Fleming, *Starting Drama Teaching* (London: David Fulton Publishers, 1994).
3 John Steptoe, *Mufaro's Beautiful Daughters* (New York: Lothrop, Lee & Shepard Books, 1987).
4 See Peter Abbs, *The Educational Imperative* (London: Falmer Press, 1994), pp. 95–112.
5 Maxine Greene, Lincoln Centre Institute for the Arts in Education, New York City, Unpublished lectures, 21 July 1994, p. 3.
6 Ibid.
7 Unpublished correspondence from workshop participant Peter Wright, University of New England.
8 Ibid.
9 Roslyn Arnold, The University of Sydney.

10 Elizabeth Darvell, The University of Tasmania.

11 Nicole Muir, The University of Melbourne.

12 Helen Fletcher, The University of Newcastle.

13 See Augusto Boal, *The Rainbow of Desire* (London: Routledge, 1995).

14 Ibid. Boal pioneered the forum or people's theatre. Although classic forum theatre depends on disenfranchised groups working through their oppressions (see Boal's, *Theatre of the Oppressed*, published by Pluto Press), the medium is powered by the spectators, or spect-actors, taking control of the theatrical space.

15 Peter Abbs, in *The Educational Imperative* (London: Falmer Press, 1994), asserted his condemnation of process drama for 'its deficiencies from an aesthetic and artistic point of view'. To argue, as Abbs does, that process drama 'rarely draws on aesthetics or on the leading theoretical literature from Aristotle's Poetics onwards' (p. 127) is puzzling given that the work of leaders, like O'Neill, is powered by a commanding knowledge of theatre and the arts disciplines.

16 John Hughes, 'Performance art, aesthetics and pedagogy: a response to Arts Education Colloquium', Unpublished correspondence to author, 1993.

17 Sally Markham, Auckland College of New Zealand.

18 Helen Fletcher.

19 Rob Galbraith. Readers are directed to further perspectives contained in H. Fletcher, 'Retrieving the mother/other from the myths and margins of O'Neill's "seal wife" drama' (*NADIE Journal*, **19**, 2, pp. 25–38); 'Letters to the Editor' (*NADIE Journal*, **20**, 1, pp. 5–10).

20 Maxine Greene, op. cit.

Chapter 3

Getting deeper: storydrama and storying
across the curriculum

Preamble

❝ *Behind David Booth's voice, we can hear the great drama story-tellers
of the century: Caldwell Cook of* The Play Way *in England, and
Winifred Ward who pioneered story and drama in the United States;
Maisie Cobby who took story and drama from Britain to Nigeria and
New Zealand; Gerry Siks and Agnes Haaga who, at the University of
Washington, created a centre for story and drama during a whole generation; Bishop E. J. Burton, T. E. ('Gerald') Tyler, Peter Slade, Brian
Way, and Dorothy Heathcote who developed the creation of stories by
children through improvisation – 'their stories.' But in David's journey, we also hear the remote voices of the Canadian pioneers who
told their tales huddled round isolated fires, sheltering against the bit-
ter winter winds and snow . . .*

*It is no wonder that storydrama is popular with modern children.
They inherit the most ancient traditions which David Booth and his
colleagues bring to them in modern guise. Then the students can
imaginatively re-tell the incidents of their own lives and the events in
contemporary media. When David is working in a classroom the
atmosphere is electric. The power of his personality and the artistic
quality of his approach codify the concentration of the whole class . . .*

*In the demonstration classes of David Booth, the children become
exemplary cases of learning how to be and do; and how to focus on a
task and see it through to completion. They activate their imaginative*

powers; and they create a living fiction which they learn to compare with reality and so order their world. But teacher-observers learn even more.

One example will serve. It was while watching David Booth at work with children in storydrama that I learned (became consciously aware of) the true nature of dramatic conflict. It was commonly said that the idea of conflict was epitomised by the Greek tragic dramatists, as explained by Aristotle: it was direct opposition of ideas. But we should remember that Greek society was infused with competition; e.g., the Olympic games and the theatrical contests. The Greek opposition was allied to competition and a warlike attitude.

This attitude is not present in David Booth's storydramas. Their conflicts are somewhat different. The alternative choices faced by the students are not direct oppositions and they do not breed competition. Their choices clash between different (but not opposite) ideas; that is, they occur between similarities as alternative solutions to a problem. The children's choices and judgements contrast with one another. They do not lead to competition and war but to cooperation, peace, love, and care for one another.

As I watched the improvisers, they concluded between them a fiduciary contract: they demonstrated a mutual trust in each other and in the storydrama. David didn't say so and nor did the children. The fiduciary contract was tacit: a sub-text agreed by them all. It was learned indirectly but learned so well that, at the end, some children were hugging each other. This form of human interaction is desperately needed as the bloodthirsty twentieth century comes to an end. David's work is a positive pointer to our mutual future.

Because David slips in and out of role so smoothly he constantly surprises students. This keeps them alert and focused because they are never quite certain of what is coming next: as in life, they are walking on a tightrope trying to adjust to the future. (Richard Courtney, 1995)

Introducing storydrama

In the above description of David Booth's praxis, the late Richard Courtney, a British-Canadian educator who was a prolific writer on drama education, notes how often the most fulfilling experiences in drama emerge when participants have a range of options from which they must choose. In the previous chapter we saw how a pre-text, when carefully selected, can yield numerous artistic possibilities for rich inquiry in the drama classroom. Now, in this chapter, readers are introduced to the power of storydrama as an artistic encounter which helps students commit to the whole curriculum. Examples from drama classrooms will be provided.

We begin with an example of drama praxis led by one of Canada's leading drama authorities, David Booth. Twenty-five drama and language teachers had enrolled in a course with Booth. The course occurred over three days and was launched with a demonstration of storydrama with a group of fourteen fifth- and sixth-graders (10–12-year-olds) from a local primary/elementary school. The teachers, a mix of primary, secondary and tertiary educators, registered for this course because they wanted to understand more about the relationship between story and drama and, also, how they could employ drama strategies to open up the world of story.

The term 'storydrama' has quite different connotations from Winifred Ward's story dramatisation. Whereas the latter implies a re-enactment of narrative, the former, storydrama, involves a more improvisatory exploration of significant themes, issues or relationships that are suggested through and by the story. 'Drama in the language classroom', Booth argues, 'is not just an activity to be used after reading a story, as a check of comprehension, or as a means of motivating children to read a particular selection.' Although drama may help in these goals it is, more importantly, a 'powerful medium' for helping children make learning happen:

> *Drama helps children journey inside the story garden, so that they can construct the symbols, images, and narrative sequence 'in action,' thus reexamining the story's ideas, experimenting with them, learning to 'play' with the narrative, and in reflection, coming to an understanding of both the story's possibilities and the art form used to create it. In drama, the mutual, symbolic collaboration of ideas, undetermined by plot allows children to pause in a fictional present, linger on an image, or move forward, backward, and sideways, in an attempt to make meaning happen. Time can be averted and ideas juxtaposed. If a narrative is being used as the source of a drama, the children can identify with and clarify what is happening both in the*

book, in the drama, and in their own lives. Learning is integrated as they engage with the symbolic art forms of both modes.[1]

The main features of storydrama can be characterised as follows:

- A concern with the issues, themes, characters, mood, conflict or spirit of the story as a beginning for dramatic exploration
- Students draw from within themselves ideas and feelings and conclusions based on the story
- The action in storydrama develops as participants solve or work through the dilemma symbolised in the story
- Improvisation that happens before, during or after the story illuminates the story while engaging the reader's imagination
- Participants are freed from the pressure of acting out the whole story or remembering a script

---

Teachers during storydrama should see themselves as:

- Questioners who awaken the students to what they wonder about the story
- Able to release students from the storyline (plot) and involve them in the roots or concepts of the story
- Facilitating student interaction with the story and with their own ideas in order to bring about meaning and so that they can reach a strong level of emotional and intellectual commitment
- Honouring the ideas the students develop
- Structuring the work so that all participants can enter the drama more deeply than they thought they could
- Artists who shape the collaborative creation of participants so that in the end all parties feel a sense of satisfaction from the work

---

> *The teacher can use the story to provide the stimulus for drama, and the story can assist the teacher in giving form to that drama. The story and its strength enable the teacher to dip into the richness of the contexts that the author has provided. Drama becomes a tool for the exploration of the ideas, relationships and language of the story. The students are not limited to the facts or words in the story, since the story per se is not the prime focus. It may indeed happen that the students' appreciation and understanding of the story deepens after drama. However, the teacher must be concerned primarily with the developmental aspects of drama that occur as the children elaborate, extend and invent. Story provides a suitable and supportive framework for building drama, enriching the quality of the dramatic experience and imparting an artistic awareness to the lives of the students involved.*[2]

As Booth's demonstration with the children became a point of reference for the participants as they grappled with the phenomenon of storydrama, and its implications for their own classroom practice, I shall unpack that work.

Storydrama: an illustration

Demonstration lessons have become an important vehicle
for illuminating drama praxis. 'When you see kids working,'
Booth maintains, 'it changes us as teachers.' Although there is an
artificiality in the circumstances and context of the demonstration,
what it does provide is an opportunity to watch a teacher at work.
'Examine what I do,' appeals Booth, 'and then be different.' Booth
resists theoretical implications that have not been driven by practical
exploration. At the heart of storydrama lies the co-construction of a
fictitious event. That co-construction depends upon the coming
together of minds and bodies and a mutual agreement to create.

Some concern has been expressed about the fallibility of
demonstration classes and their cultivation of uncharacteristic
exemplars. Ironically, these concerns are voiced usually by academic
theorists who appear uninterested in subjecting their own ideas on
educational practice to the unpredictable occurrences in classrooms.[3]
Working with children immediately grounds ideas in the real world
of teachers, children and their schools. There is now compelling
evidence that teachers learn best from other teachers, and seem more
able to effect change as they interact with and learn from credible
mentors. Teacher education programmes, for instance, are being
restructured to provide for more internships in schools where
student-teachers can have greater access to actual classroom
practitioners. Few teacher-educators appear to work frequently in
school classrooms. David Booth is one exception.

Although the source on which the following practice is based is
familiar to Booth, he, nonetheless, has not met these children before.
Booth knows that the constraints of demonstration – e.g. many adults
watching, children unfamiliar with the teacher, working in a foreign
land (in this instance, Australia) and classroom – may undermine
the work and its fulfilling execution. However, these constraints
fuel the storydrama with an edge or risk that is at the core of his
approach. It would be unlikely that most of the educators watching
the demonstration have subjected their own teaching to such public
scrutiny and it is clearly a moment of interest for them to witness an
experienced practitioner willing to share his evolving artistry.

Artistry is powered by risk-taking.

A number of sources have been cited to reconstruct the following storydrama: these include, transcripts of the storydrama, Booth's analysis which incorporates his past writing, the teachers' responses, and my own linking commentary.

Constructing a puzzlement

In Chapter 1 we saw how storydrama is generated when the focusing story, *The True Story of the Three Little Pigs*, contains what Booth refers to as a puzzlement. A puzzlement might occur because of an uncertainty within the text, a fascination, an event or detail which has not been fully explored. Drawing on Aidan Chambers'[4] four questions of readers: What did you like about the story? What did you not like in the story? What puzzled you? How can we take those puzzlements, connect and explore them?, Booth knows that his task in the early stages of his drama praxis is to arrest the attention of the children and focus their interest on constructing an engaging puzzlement.

After the children enter, their nervous energy is revealed as they sit some distance from Booth. He moves closer to them. 'I'm from Canada', he says to these Australian children. 'Who knows anything about my country?' There is a refreshing wit to Booth's repartee with the children. Immediately, they feel at ease and share their impressions of Canadian baseball, and contrast the Canadian and Australian national anthems. When the children laugh at Booth's response that Waltzing Matilda is Australia's anthem, he asks one girl, 'Have you ever met Matilda?' When another girl quips, 'My sister has a friend called Matilda', Booth replies, 'Is she the one who waltzes?' The sardonic edge to the teacher's interaction keeps the students intrigued and seems to reassure them that they won't be treated as fools; nor will he.

When Booth asks whether the children would like to test his knowledge about Australia, one boy, Bob,[5] asks, 'Who are our indigenous people?' Booth is surprised with this question as it relates directly to the drama work. 'Our work today is about the first people in a land, Bob,' he contemplates, then adds, 'you have opened my lesson for me.'

The picture story, 'The Expedition', launches the storydrama.[6] The pictures focus on a band of marauding soldiers who invade an island, plunder a temple, retreat to their boat with their spoils, a stone temple, only to discover that their own steam engine has been stolen by the island's inhabitants and placed in the position where the islanders' temple used to be. Booth knows that behind the pictures there are rich stories to be explored about the soldiers and the inhabitants: What motivates the soldiers to plunder? Why does the picture book not show who the inhabitants are? What would the soldiers do with the temple now? Why are the inhabitants so clever and resourceful? What does this storybook teach us about authority, greed, and ownership?

 Using the ideas of the story as cues for their own dramatic responses allows children to test the implications of what is written and of their own responses. As teacher, I can draw upon the vast resources of the story as a way of stimulating and enriching their search for meaning in drama. Groups can test and clarify the implications of the text collectively, so that each person can see the difference in the various perceptions and interpretations, and can then make decisions about his or her own responses.[7]

'Who are the people who had the temple originally?' asks Booth, after all the pictures have been seen.

'The natives', replies one boy.

'Let's call them indigenous people', he suggests. 'So these indigenous people lived on this island quite a long time ago from the look of things. And do you know anything about these people? Do you know anything about their behaviour, about what they did? Robert?'

'I don't know', muses Robert.

'That's right,' confirms Booth, 'we didn't see them once in the whole book.'

'They're pretty smart', says Noel.

'Yes, they are pretty smart, because we didn't see them. What else did they do that demonstrates their cleverness?' asks Booth.

'They knew that the temple would be nicked,' reflects Noel, 'so they nicked the ship's.'

'Can I ask a question?' responds the teacher. 'Were they fair?'

'Yes', replies Mick.

'That's pretty strong, Mick. You think they were fair?'

'Yeah!'

'Why?' queries the teacher.

'Well,' Mick begins, 'somebody took theirs, so it's…'

'So,' interjects Booth, 'if someone steals something of yours, you can steal something of theirs?'

'Yeah,' confirms Mick, 'equal.'

'I wonder what the police would think of that', retorts Booth: 'if somebody steals your bike you can steal their bike.'

'Not exactly like that', replies Mick. 'This is different, 'cause there's no laws for that.'

'There's no laws for temple stealing?' asks Booth.

'Yeah, there is', corrects Mick.

'Nah, not really', replies another.

'These people,' says Robert, 'they didn't care.'

'They took their plans', elaborates Deb, 'that they probably worked hard on a lot.'

'So, it would depend on whose law, would it?' questions Booth.

'Yes', respond the students.

'In our drama today,' poses the teacher, 'would you rather be the invisible people or the people who stole the temple? You can vote.' (Booth raises his hand.) 'Who would rather be the people we don't see?' (Ten students have raised their hands while the other four have voted to be the 'invaders'.)

The discussion on the story focuses initially on the indigenous peoples. This focus seems teacher-directed and led to one adult observer later commenting that had Booth engineered the culminating vote by asking first *Who would prefer to be the people who stole the temple?*, the drama might have taken quite a different path. Booth agreed with this observation, noting that drama teachers develop their own tricks and are conscious of what they can achieve within limited time constraints.

Like O'Neill, Booth is not bashful about promoting the teacher as an active accomplice in the children's play. 'When teachers control the quality of the learning,' he suggests, 'rather than controlling the content, they will enable students to become meaning makers, constructing real meanings for themselves, exploring the significance of the dramatic events that make up the curriculum.'

The children have voted. 'So,' continues Booth, 'for today we'll begin by being those people. We know little about them, but we know one thing: You had a temple, you used it, you valued it, and when it was gone, you rebuilt it with whatever you could find.'

The teacher suggests to the group that they will move ahead in time by a hundred years, and that he will come back to visit them. 'You're going to have some kind of person to speak to me as leader', he asserts. 'I don't know how you choose your leaders. I don't know if they're men or women. I'm going to turn my back and let you decide whom you want to be leader, whom you want to speak to me.' Booth turns his back while the group decides on Deb. Booth checks with Deb that she has accepted this leadership responsibility. 'The leader does not have to speak,' says Booth, 'the leader may be so powerful that she has lesser people to speak for her. So you have choices, Deb, you are safe. Maybe the leader is never seen.'

Deb wonders whether her people would 'kick up a big fuss' about the stolen temple. 'Well, you might,' replies Booth, 'or you might not care anymore.' Another student asks if their people speak English. Booth suggests that although a hundred years ago no English was spoken he will be able to speak their language, even though it is in another dialect.

The teacher has a strong investment in these opening moments. The teacher while interacting with and assisting the students in their endeavour to enter the artform, is simultaneously controlling the quality of the experience. For instance, the movement into the future and selection of a student leader is initiated by the teacher. 'Dramatic artistry grows', argues Booth, 'from an understanding based on experience – where the heart, the mind, the spirit are struggling at once to see bigger pictures, more complex frameworks, wider connections to self and situations.' The trick is to find an entry point to the drama of sufficient interest to the group and to make decisions which can support that interest. While the group selected Deb to be leader, Booth consciously offers her support by suggesting that she might not, for instance, have to speak.

> *The artist works from an informed yet formless hunch when seeking a core of entry.*

Experiencing the puzzlement

Fundamental to Booth's work in storydrama is the frequency in which he assumes a role. It would be an unusual event if no teacher role-play occurred in Booth's storydrama. As Courtney indicated in the Preamble, Booth's powerful personality inevitably results in his adaptation of quite strong roles. 'I work strongly', Booth claims, 'because I am always short of time and the boys respond immediately.' Ironically, it was a girl, Deb, who was an immediate equal match for Booth's role play in the opening moments of 'The Expedition' drama:

'People,' states Booth, in role, to the children, 'thank you for coming to greet me.' While pointing behind him, he adds, 'I shall make the other men wait in the boat, in the launch.' The students do not respond to this suggestion of a force waiting in the rear. Instead, some students bow to him. 'I appreciate your kindness in bowing to me,' he responds, 'but I want you to stand and be on equal terms with me. I come as one who asks forgiveness. Who is your leader? I have come to return your temple.'

'And that's supposed to make everything better now', retorted Deb.

'No, it's to remove guilt from my country. We are trying to make amends. On the ship, out of your view, I have the temple in pieces with architects and designers who will reconstruct it flawlessly and give you back what you lost.'

'Why did you take our pride and joy in the first place?' quizzes Deb.

'I apologise for having come from a nation who saw that as their duty. I was not born then, and we have learned so much.' (Some boys in the rear whisper and point at Booth.)

'Why do you return it after all these years?' continued Deb. 'It's like you kept it for just as long as you could look at it. Is there any damage to our temple?'

'The temple', the visitor explained, 'was taken apart stone by stone and taken to my country. We have brought these stones back to be re-built. You must understand that in my country we re-built your temple, we used it.'

'In the same style?' Deb asked.

'We do not know how you used it here. We had to use it in our own way. But we have cleaned it up, taken it apart, brought it back, and we're going to rebuild it on your island for you. It is our gift.'

'May I please have a conference with my people?' directs Deb. (Her people gather around and whisper inaudibly.)

'Excuse me leader,' interjects Booth, 'you will notice that I have come unarmed and my launch is unarmed. However, the ship around the harbour is heavily armed.' (While Booth talks some of the people whisper, 'Skin him'. Deb says, 'Ssssh' in reply.) 'I'm sorry, but I must return and it's getting dark. I shall return in the morning.'

'We want to see our temple,' asserts Deb, 'to see if it's all right.'

'I shall return it in the morning,' repeats Booth, 'with that information for you. I appreciate your kindness and I shall leave you with this tiny gift for when I return.' (Booth offers an imaginary gift in his cupped hands.) 'Take this gift, open your hand.' (Deb refuses.) 'You don't want the gift?'

'Can I please know what it is before you give it to me?'

'Yes,' replies the stranger, 'it is a medal from my ruler for the leader of your people. Do you want the medal?' (The people confer.) 'You wish it?' (He hands it over.) 'You may hold the medal as a symbol of my ruler's honour. I'll be back in twenty-four hours with the temple. Thank you.' (He turns away and then steps out of role.)

'Let's see', Booth says. He suggests the children sit, 'You're a pretty strong tribe here, aren't you?' Booth then reflects on the work with them.

Booth conceded later that he was surprised that a girl had been elected leader. 'Traditionally in drama,' he mused, 'the boys work the first half hour and the girls work the second half hour and if the drama is poor in the first half hour then the girls never enter.' This response generates some disagreement, with one teacher asserting that in Australian primary education the girls, in his experience, 'take the lead'. 'In North America,' Booth replied, 'the girls will take the stance that is right and neat but they won't handle the problems initially.' In this classroom context the social health of the group was such that the group could accept Deb in the leadership role. For example, Deb is firm with the visitor: the teacher in role. She does not accept his excuses readily, ignores his threats, and is suspicious of the peace-offering.

When the students reflected, they confirmed their suspicion of the visitor. The temple, they believed, was a fake, and would have no spiritual significance for them now. When Booth suggested that they return to the drama, and, in the same role, presented the group with the 'authentic plans' of the temple, these were rejected out of hand as fraudulent. Booth stepped out of role when threatened by the group.

'You have to stop the drama', Booth later admitted, 'when the group is going to kill you.' This group of children is united in its belief that the visitor, who represents those who plundered the people, should be made to suffer a similar loss and deprivation. Booth briefly re-enters the drama and advises the people, through Deb, that they should 'not take the temple'. This advice seems peculiar to Deb given that she has previously rejected the temple as unauthentic and non-spiritual.

> The teacher-in-role strategy is the artistry of storydrama because it enables the teacher to accompany the children into the metaphoric world of the story.

Tensions and goose-bump drama

In storydrama, the teacher is not providing the students with simple solutions to life problems. Although the children in 'The Expedition' drama have decided not to take the temple, Booth's reading of history teaches him that indigenous cultures throughout time have endured the indignity of usurpation and dislocation. The islanders have been threatened twice by an invading army, once when their temple was originally pillaged, and now by the invaders' successors who are determined that the temple be returned. In an ideal world the islanders might ignore these hostile overtures, but the drama confirms the real presence of the marauders. The task for the children is to seek logical decisions based on immediate confrontation.

> *As children explore through conversation and role play – interacting, listening, speaking – they learn to risk and to express. These are necessary experiences on the road to literacy. Children explore life through their own storying and through the stories of others, creating their own unique narratives, their own ways of representing yesterday, today and tomorrow. They require broad, thoughtful experience with real situations to learn how to read the world intellectually, physically, emotionally, spiritually.*[8]

Booth's line, 'Do not take the temple', creates an immediate tension for the people as it contradicts the visitor's previous position. Booth exploits this tension further when he asks the adults in the room to stand and to take one step towards the children. The adults become the visitor's army and a heavy-handed threat is now given, 'We will give you back the temple and you have until the sun goes down to accept it.' Deb, still firm, refuses this offer, and the pressure is applied for a decision to be made. Robert, another student, suggests that his people call their god for advice.

One boy, Sam, assumes the role of the god and confirms that the temple is a fraud. He urges that the islanders avoid brutality but that they send a delegation of three representatives to the visitor's ship. The adult army stands again and Booth, layering in another tension, whispers to Deb that the delegation should not go on the ship. In a splendidly caught web, Deb now rethinks the delegates' mission, fears treachery, and insists that she speaks with her people. Deb is constantly checking out strategy with her fellow islanders. When the visitor returns alone, the children exploit this opportunity by capturing him, claiming that he is a traitor and that they need to find out more information from him.

Booth appears caught off guard by this decision, calls for time-out where he can probe the children's thinking. What follows now is perhaps one of the most illuminating interactions between a teacher and his students on what is happening in their storydrama:

DAVID: I was just realising how absolutely brave you are as a tribe to take me captive again, because, of course, you have all of them waiting at sundown, don't you? Do you think they won't move on you if you have me? Is that it?

DEB: Well, you have to be important because you . . .

DAVID: [*Challenging*] Oh, really? I have to be important? What if I'm their pawn? What if I have been sent to you by them? What if I'm not important at all? What if you've just been condemned to death? What if I've told you everything? What if I don't know anymore? How are you going to make me 'spill my guts' as you say? You're the one who imprisoned me.

PAUL: Well, you could go back and get more information for us.

DAVID: You want me to spy for you? Why should I spy for you?

ROBERT: [*Contemplative*] This whole story is pouring into different compartments.

DAVID: It is, so what do we make of these different compartments? How do we make sense of it?

ROBERT: I don't know. I'm just telling everyone before it goes too far.

DAVID: But I'm the teacher. I don't have to have these ideas, you have to have the ideas. You have to solve it. What if your tribe doesn't have any more ideas? What if your tribe is 'idea-ed' out? You've captured this person, he's back, you're going to bring the god back. You're going to torture him again, take him through the trip again? He is already on your side. He said, 'Don't take the temple.' What is it that you're going to do with him?

A feature of the above interchange is the rapid inquisitive banter between teacher and students. The teacher is searching for a logical reason as to why the students have kidnapped the visitor again. He challenges the children to become spectators to their own action and note the implications of their behaviour. They, too, challenged him to understand the legitimacy of their action. Booth has likened this moment to 'goose-bump teaching', where the classroom leader is arrested, emotionally and intellectually, by the participants' responses:

 I notice my own goose bumps appearing at the oddest moments in teaching, when a youngster in the class speaks briefly yet stops the action in the room for a milli-second, when the class becomes silent out of respect for their own work, when the young actors coalesce with the directed energy of an ensemble. Tiny moments that only

teachers recognise, teachers who must remember to cover their arms, lest the rest of the world notice the goose bumps.[9]

When Bob proposes that Booth is hypnotised by the islanders, the children begin to make a case that their people have spiritual strength:

> ROBERT: [To Booth] *What do you know about us? How do you know we don't have the strength?*
> BOOTH: *I don't know that.*
> STEVEN: *There could be more people hiding.*
> BOOTH: *So, you . . . aren't all of your people on the land.*
> SAM: *We could have fifty FBI agents hiding in the trees.*
> BOOTH: *Ah, you can't do that because that would destroy the drama. We've already worked through who you are. But you could have more people, I would allow that.*
> MICK: *Maybe the temple that we've got from the boat has got firearms so we could go up there and shell them all down . . .*
> BOOTH: *What is it, Mick, that you want to do with the gun powder you stole from the old boat . . . that you have hidden in the temple?*
> MICK: *If you start an attack on us we could have people at the temple and if they see anyone get hurt then they could shoot.*
> BOOTH: *But in a war, where you have gun powder, and they have guns, I think people will die. I think maybe as the leader, Deb, you would not want this to happen. [Challenging Deb] Can you not stop what Mick has suggested, which is using firepowder on the people? If you can't, you can't.*
> DEB: *I don't think we could stop them. How do you know that we do not have an army hidden everywhere?*
> ROBERT: [Over the others' agreement] *Hiding!*
> BOOTH: *Well, I don't, but it's odd that you imprisoned me before and told me the story, and it's odd that you called upon your god and not upon your guards. So I don't think you do.*
> SAM: *How do you know that we called on our god?*
> BOOTH: *Because I was in the dream wasn't I?*
> SAM: *You weren't supposed to know about it.*
> BOOTH: *So, can you give amnesia to the person? Can you take away his memory?*

Booth is swayed by the students' logic and their conviction. 'You've got me in your control again', he conceded. 'You've brought me back here and I've warned you twice, "Don't take the temple!" ' Booth relinquishes his command over the drama and submits to the students' direction. The discussion concludes when he agrees with the children that the strongest witch doctor in the community will hypnotise him in an attempt to uncover why the islanders should not take the temple.

The beckoning future is controlled by the actions of the present informed by the past. **The teachers' artistry helps the students confront their actions' implications**.

Subjugation and culmination

❦ *Why do some critics feel that drama as a learning medium is deficient from an aesthetic and artistic point of view? Young people exploring issues are not simply looking for information and answers as if making a salt-and-flour topical map. Why do such critics not believe in aesthetic, metaphoric, spiritual and cognitive responses to issues that concern us? Do they really think that the participants don't know they are in a fictive, imagined 'as if' context? Do they assume that the participants aren't aware of the strategies and techniques that are being employed within the dramatic playing experience? What Peter Abbs calls 'the inhibitions, blocks and anxieties that stand in the way of a profound systematic reclamation of aesthetic education' may simply be the revengeful gatherings of those adults who have felt left out, passed over, or who rage at the night. All of this has the aura of those conspiracy theories, the ones of intrigue that spring up about anything we can't or don't want to comprehend. I am so saddened by the attack on the term 'educational drama,' as if the term 'education' is a negative descriptor on the arts processes. Of course we who work in schools are concerned with educating young people – people who have been excluded from the cultural arts of the past, people who could find no means of adding their voices, their heritage, their communities to the great arts of the influential. I teach young people in prison, in ghettos, and in suburbia, surrounded by cement plazas and highways. What is their art? Where is it hiding?*[10]

Artists, Maxine Greene reminds us, are for disclosing the extraordinary in the ordinary. They distort the commonplace and affirm the work of imagination. 'They are for doing all this in such a way', she muses, 'as to enable those who open themselves to what they create to see more, to hear more, to feel more, to attend to more facets of the experienced world.'[11] Booth seems to adopt Greene's words as his *modus operandi*. The students have earned the power they now wield, they have held their ground, and successfully presented a case on why the islanders would dare to venture a second kidnapping. In the process, they are finding their voice, transforming the action, and discovering their ability to manipulate the dramatic artform.

The teacher in role has been subjugated. He has been conquered by the islanders who now probe his mind for the damaging information it might contain. The children have selected the most timid girl in the class, Susan, to embody the one who transfixes, the all-powerful one who can mitigate time and mind. They will suggest questions for Susan to ask Booth while he is in the hypnotic trance. Ironically, Susan's face is hidden by her hair fringe, an actual reminder of her isolated and withdrawn place in this group, a fact later confirmed by her classroom teacher who seemed mesmerised by Susan's uncharacteristic posturing.

'Sit down', she tells the visitor while launching this final phase of the storydrama. As he submits to her request, the other children sit while Susan stands. 'What do you know about the temple?' she asks. 'Why do you think and say we shouldn't take it?' The visitor, now placid, answers in riddles. 'The temple is real and a fraud', he recites. 'Within the stones are the voices of your people and they say to give you the temple, but also within the stones are the voices of my people.' The group are whispering among themselves and help Susan find the question which will most reveal the visitor's mission. She listens as the questions are whispered to her and selects those which she believes will reveal the truth.

The artistry of Booth's roleplay here is that again he makes the students work at finding the meaning. While the visitor has softened and developed a less intense tone than in the earlier part of the drama, the students struggle knowing that there is no saccharine solution to the storydrama:

'Why are you giving it back after all these years?' asks Susan.
'We need', parrots Booth, 'to put something on your island to control this area.'
'Why do you want the island?'
'We need to control the ocean.'
'But why do you need to control the ocean?'
'We need a base here.'
'But why this island?'
'Because this island lies between the two great lands.'

> 'Which two great lands?'
> 'The two great lands to the east and to the west.'
> 'What happens if we do accept it?'
> 'You will have your temple back and we will have your island for a base.'
> 'What kind of a base?'
> 'I am not to tell you this.'
> 'Is it a base for war?'
> 'Yes.'
> 'Against who?'
> 'Against any enemy?'
> 'Why do you need enemies when you can have friends?'

The visitor confirms the suspicions of the islanders: their temple has been vilified and might be an instrument of their own destruction. This information corroborates their hunch. They terminate the hypnosis, refuse the temple for a third time, and live with the fear that their community's maxim, 'What is the use of having enemies when we can all be friends?', will be of no use given a conquering aggressor.

'When I began this lesson', Booth admitted to the children at the close of their drama, 'I did not know what I know now.' He confides in them that the weapons of mass destruction contained within the temple's stones were created through their work. 'You drew from me this strange story', contemplated the teacher in recognition of the power of context in storydrama. Booth, by responding to and accepting the ideas of these children, has transformed them from passive actors into dynamic players.

Interestingly enough, these students' regular classroom teacher, who watched the demonstration, commented on this amelioration, especially with Susan during the trance episode. 'A particular pleasure for me', he reflected, 'was to observe a rather shy and self-conscious girl confront and question David in a way that was both determined and assertive.' He highlighted the value of the process and how it compelled his students to think in action. 'I would see this as a pretty powerful tool you've got here and I've never seen it used this way', he asserted. The storydrama demonstration was to inspire a significant change in this teacher's practice as he began to contemplate a new artistic pedagogy:

> *I was staggered by what the kids came up with . . . they identified with . . . well . . . the issues, the period, but they identified with the um . . .*

they're sort of placed in the situation where they actually begin to live the situation. Rather than read about it, they're sort of . . . they're part of it. They're not removed from it, they're actually involved with it. Now, to get that level of involvement . . . can really make a sort of peak learning experience. And I haven't done that before. I really haven't seen it done before . . .

He had seen his students in a new light and had come closer to comprehending what constituted a peak learning experience. These observations stand as a fine rebuttal for the detractors of process drama who demand evidence of its power.

> *The artist teaches new ways of seeing and encourages new ways of trying.*

Characteristics of the artistry in pre-text and storydrama:
- Selecting a pre-text which contains the seeds of inquiry
- Raising possibilities rather than confirming probabilities
- Helping participants attend to the moment
- Developing a sense of community
- Releasing the participants from the predetermined constraint of character portrayal
- Informed by a rich understanding of the dramatic artform
- Selecting strategies that pursue engagement and detachment
- Seeking a form which enables participants to reveal their relationship to the event
- Inviting participants to co-create the text based on their desires, needs and agendas
- Claims the power of the imagination to transcend consciousness and being
- Powered by risk-taking
- Working from an informed yet formless hunch when seeking a core of entry
- Drawing on the teacher-in-role strategy because it accompanies the children into the metaphoric world of the story
- Helping the students confront their actions' implications
- Teaching new ways of seeing and encouraging new ways of trying

In the next section, we shall read how the these characteristics of artistry, which are central to pretext and storydrama, can be adapted across the curriculum.

Drama praxis and storying across the curriculum

❝ *He seemed suspicious to me though because he didn't ask us for our password he just stood there and I waited for us to say our oath . . . I was thinking to myself what Will had said he told us to be very care- ful not to let the torres find out so I was wondering to myself if he found out and killed him. But I couldn't accuse him or approach him yet. I had to find out more about him.* (Thirteen-year-old Meryl's log entry)

The predicament which Meryl describes above occurred during a social studies lesson where she and her class mates had assumed the roles of eighteenth-century American patriots in Boston. In their drama, the students were expecting the teacher to assume the role of the patriots' leader who had convened a secretive meeting of revolutionaries planning tactics to overthrow the British, known as the Tories in Meryl's log (hence 'torres' above). However, the patriots were surprised when their leader assumed a threatening attitude, and resisted their tactics. Meryl's log entry captures the difficulty her class had in reading the motives of this 'suspicious' man. In her words, they 'had to find out more about him' before deciding upon an appropriate course of action.

Although this session took place in the contexts of a lesson where historical investigation was the focus, the children and teacher were clearly working in a story mode. For the remainder of this chapter, I will demonstrate how 'storying', as Gordon Wells (1986) describes it, is crucial to students' active engagement with curriculum, and how drama praxis helps students commit to the curriculum. We have previously seen in my discussion of David Booth's praxis how working within a story framework can release students from the deadly constraints of much classroom presentation and liberate them in their questioning and exploration of curricula issues. I will now map out how drama praxis helps students develop into critical language learners able to construct a sense of themselves and the world in which they live.

The denial of children's stories

I plan to use an example from the social studies classroom to illuminate the potential that drama praxis has for cross-curricula investigation. Rarely, does it seem to me, do teachers in social studies consider the rich possibilities that drama praxis presents to them when facilitating student commitment to curriculum.

Social studies educators share with all curriculum specialists a desire to make learning experiences relevant to students' lives. Unfortunately, much social studies education has been characterised by the conventional transmitter–receiver teaching model where students have been passive recipients of the stories of others.

Researchers have suggested, for instance, that at every grade level most students find social studies to be one of the least interesting and most irrelevant subjects in the curriculum (see Giroux and McLaren, 1993; Shaughnessy and Haladyna, 1985). They cite reasons such as dull content and unexciting teacher presentations. What is particularly disturbing about these responses is that research conducted early in the twentieth century elicited the same result (Stevens, 1912). Social studies teachers, according to Stevens, dominated most classroom discourse, sought and rewarded correct factual responses, and paid little attention to helping students become self-reliant and independent learners. Fifty years later, Floyd Hunkins agreed with this analysis. He found that teachers asked over 90 per cent of the questions in class, most of these questions checking the recall of facts, 'not to stimulate thinking, nor to guide pupils in developing effective inquiry techniques' (Hunkins, 1969, p. 61). I wonder whether the twenty-first century will yield contrary data if, as Hume and Wells (1999) argue, published social studies curriculum rarely invites teachers and students to confront multiple and shifting perspectives.

The problem with most curriculum programmes has been the emphasis placed on mastery of information. For the most part in social studies education this emphasis has relegated students into powerless positions where other people's stories dominate classroom discourse. Rather than help students struggle with the contradictory forces operating in society throughout time, social studies curricula have developed into sets of isolated facts to memorise with no relation to present life needs.

The denial of students' own storying capacities seems odd to me given that social studies is characterised by the narratives of time. In social studies, students are constantly searching, inventing and reinventing a view of the world as they attempt to formulate their own truthful account of it. As Giroux (1988) reminds us, the quest for knowledge requires students 'to learn how to be able to move outside of their own frame of reference so that they can question the legitimacy of a given fact, concept or issue' (p. 63). Like John Dewey before him, Giroux has appealed for pedagogical structures which help students develop multiple perspectives on events so that they can build well-informed and grounded interpretations. We are beginning to see how storydrama provides a framework where our students can enter into a collaborative narrative which constantly transforms and grows. Students can become the generators of their own knowledge and experience how events can determine and shape human action.

'We all have our own unique stories,' Barton and Booth (1990, p. 14) tell us, 'our own ways of storying, our own ways of representing what is, what was, and what might be.' In my own teaching I have deliberately drawn on the power of story in helping students develop ownership of the work. Common sense dictates that those who tell or enact stories have formulated their own way of organising human experience. When Meryl wonders to herself how she should read the attitude of the suspicious person, she is beginning to story about and categorise human action. How does storying help in this categorisation?, and how can teachers' drama praxis permit students control of their own learning?

Planning curriculum

I was working with a group of Grade 7 students who were studying an American pre-revolutionary event known as the Boston Massacre. On the day of the massacre, 5 March 1770, British soldiers had reputedly slaughtered five colonists in Boston. Sam Adams, a well-known patriot of the time, argued that this incident was further evidence of the ruthless and bloody-minded intent of the British. My own reading of this event had indicated that the soldiers were incited by a mob to shoot and, in fact, saw themselves as victims not persecutors. Here, I thought, was an array of conceptual issues worthy of exploration: How do we arrive at a truthful version of the events? Whose cause, the patriots or the soldiers, has greater claim? What does the Boston Massacre communicate to seventh-graders today?

One of my students, Albert, had borrowed a children's book from his local library describing the massacre. This text, *The Story of the Boston Massacre* (Phelan, 1976), opened with the plans of influential patriot leaders, such as Sam and John Adams, Paul Revere and William Molineux, who had just learned that 10,000 British soldiers were about to enter Boston harbour. A secret patriots' meeting was being arranged where the 'Whig' sympathisers could discuss the growing 'Tory' menace. I followed a hunch and decided to read some sections of the book aloud to the class as a pre-text to dramatic activity.

Creating a learning environment

'Sam Adams', I began to read to the seventh-graders, 'slips from the group at the Bunch of Grapes tavern beckoning his fellow patriot Will Molineux to follow him.' I attempted to colour my reading with an atmosphere of urgency and mystery. 'Once outside the taproom,' I continued in a lowered voice, 'Adams whispers that the news [of the soldiers' arrival] is not unexpected, still their closest associates should be alerted. There are decisions to be made this very night. Molineux is in agreement and offers his home as a meeting place.' I asked the class to think of a message which Adams might have sent to his patriot friends. The room was busy with the networking of messages. The students' interest seemed baited. They were beginning to tell a story.

'If you were going to attend William Molineux's house that night,' I interjected before the networking ceased, 'what route do you think you would take in Boston?'

NADIA: *I would go through little alleys where no one could see me . . . With something covering my face.*

PHIL: *Yes . . . no one could see you.*

TOM: *Once in a while look to see if anyone was following you.*

PHIL: *I wonder why you wouldn't want anyone to know where you were going?*

NADIA: *Because if one of the soldiers saw that you were going there they would get suspicious and tell all the rest of the soldiers and then they'd attack you.*

PHIL: *You would be in fear.*

JESSICA: *Well if it wasn't a soldier . . . and just a person and they said 'where are you going?' . . . and they might be like undercover . . . and so attack.*

PHIL: *So to be a patriot in those days it must have been . . .*

NADIA: *Sneaky.*

MERYL: *Dangerous.*

PHIL: *Some risk involved in being a patriot.*

TOM: *And you would want to know how to keep a secret.*

PHIL: [Contemplatively] *You would need to know how to keep a secret . . . Would you like to reconstruct what it might have been like to be a patriot attending that meeting?* [They do][12]

Their reading of the text suggested a 'cloak and dagger' quality in a patriot's life; they had focused on the risks involved. Not only would a patriot have to exercise caution walking through the streets of Boston, but he or she would need to be trustworthy and courageous. Quite subtly, I was hoping to endow the students with the role of patriots who might have attended that meeting at Molineux's. The students were beginning to enter the story through their telling of it.

From the inside looking out

We saw previously how in David Booth's approach to drama praxis students are actively creating their own version of events. Students are agreeing to participate as if the story were true. When working within the domain of story students can check and confirm their understanding of events and confront the perceptions of others. As Booth argues:

 The context of drama allows children in role to initiate language interaction and wield authority, and they have opportunities to gain understandings from their own frames of reference, free from the language expectations and control of the teacher. Learning opportunities are altered by changes in the relationship between teacher and children. As students interact inside role, they are able to explore social functions of language that may not arise in the language forms of the traditional classroom. The context plays a part in determining what they say, and what they say plays a part in determining the context.

(Booth, 1987, p. 7)

'Where do you think William Molineux lives?' was the question I put to the seventh-graders after they had jointly drawn a huge map of Boston in 1770. The students, standing in front of the map, surveyed places of interest we had marked. The question, I hoped, would help put them on the inside of the story rather than remain a commentator on it. 'On the lower end of Marlborough Street,' Nadia suggested, 'by the Liberty Tree.' The students seemed to like the idea the Molineux would live near the Liberty Tree. Nadia then wrote an 'X' on the map to indicate Molineux's house.

'Now,' I proceeded, 'if we are going to attend this meeting at Molineux's we have to get there first.' Taking a different coloured marker each student then located a place on the map where he or she lived. As they were contemplating and recording possibilities, I noted aloud some of the patriots' abodes. 'Nadia lives on Lynn Street', I observed. 'Jessica lives over on North Square. Joyce in front of the Old State House. Susan over near Faneuil Hall and Meryl on

Sunbury Street.' They seemed to be enjoying discussing the various street names and noting the different sites.

'In your own colour,' I suggested, 'draw the route you took on that dark and lonely night to Molineux's house.' With a hive of activity, the group excitedly applied marker to paper. I noticed Amara had drawn a heartbeat type route just before arriving at the Liberty Tree. 'Those are alleys', she quietly said, noticing my interest. 'I went back around my steps through the alleys.' 'She doesn't want anyone to follow her', Teddy added. Most of the journeys had now been drawn. 'You are all taking different routes', I observed. Unusual patterns were noticed. 'Most people live on the westside', Teddy argued. 'We live in groups', retorted Tom. 'Except for Joyce,' I noticed, 'who is located roughly in the centre of town all by herself. Where might her loyalties lie?' There seemed to be a contemplative pause after I raised that question. The children's roles were beginning to assume shape.

The landscape was being filtered with potential stories. Neighbours were located and places of interest discussed. 'It's all very relaxing and peaceful,' Albert later wrote of his neighbourhood, 'but sometimes the British soldiers come around and we would all be very quiet and look mean and menacing.' Menacing seemed to describe aptly the journeys which the patriots took that evening. 'I realised that someone was following, so I walked faster to Cow Lane,' Amara wrote in her journal, 'and I looked back and saw a shadow . . . It was only a cat.' Other patriots' journeys were dangerous too. 'It was cold and dreary', echoed Nadia. 'I left the house, clenching my penguin pass . . . I used a different route to get there, taking allies [*sic*] and underground passes.' Penguin was a password that the group thought the patriots might use to enter Molineux's.

Confronting tension and dilemma

A distinguishing feature of drama praxis is that students have to work their way through action and endure the tension faced during this action. Narrative structure does not necessarily contain such tension. Although the seventh-graders had begun to enter the storyworld of the Boston patriots, and encountered some of the language and commitment prevalent in this world, in my mind they had not assumed any responsibility of a patriot or explored the costs of a patriot's life. How could I press into our work a probe which would challenge the group to confront themselves and the world they inhabited? Merely telling a story was not a sufficient probe.

The map had been a useful precursor to providing a context to the work experienced, but it was not until the group prepared oaths of honour which the patriots might share at the Molineux meeting that a powerful dilemma became clear to me: How might loyal patriots react when faced with a disloyal patriot? If I was to assume the role of someone other than Molineux, perhaps a spy or traitor, I might usefully test the commitment of the patriots during the meeting. 'You won't recognise who I am', I mentioned to the four groups of patriots as they were preparing to make their way down a makeshift alleyway we had constructed in the classroom.

'The patriots made their way to William Molineux's house', I began to narrate. Teddy, Albert and Amara were the first to negotiate cautiously a path through the desks. 'Their journey to the Liberty Tree', I continued, 'had been long and difficult.' Albert was deviously clutching what looked like a weapon, while constantly looking over his shoulder. Teddy had drawn a sign, 'No Lobsterbacks', which he held in front of his chest. As they arrived at the door, Amara, holding a toy penguin, knocked three times. The stranger opened it. 'The Penguin', whispered Amara holding up the animal, 'GAWKS', continued Teddy, 'at midnight', completed Albert, while Amara furtively tapped the penguin on his rifle three times. It was richly theatrical, aptly conveying aspects of the underworld which they felt the patriots inhabited. It seemed that for this group at least the previous steps were a useful precursor to the meeting.

When all the patriots had entered the house and had said their oaths I invited them to share their plans for dealing with the British soldiers, who were known as 'the red menace' or 'the lobsterbacks' because of their blood-coloured coats:

 Teddy: We should put tar on them.
Madelene: And then feather them.
Phil: They might fight back if we put tar on them.
Meryl: Well, there's no reason why we can't fight them.
Phil: They have guns you know.
Meryl: So do we.
Phil: Are you saying we should be violent with them?
Meryl: Well, they're violent with us.
Phil: I don't really see what purpose putting tar on their backs is going to achieve.

> MERYL: *Well, we have to do something given what they have been doing.*
>
> PHIL: *What have they done to us these soldiers? They've done nothing to me personally. Have they done anything to you?*
>
> TEDDY: *They kicked and whipped my brother.*
>
> PHIL: *Was he putting tar on their backs?*
>
> TEDDY: *They've got savage minds.*
>
> PHIL: *So you think they're pretty violent.*
>
> ALBERT: *They taxed my bullets.*
>
> PHIL: *So? I mean a few taxes isn't going to hurt. Violence is . . .*
>
> MERYL: *What have you got against violence?*

The transcript moves from a consideration of tactics to a questioning of the host's motivations. Meryl's suspicions mount given the host's seeming duplicity. As I continued to assume a threatening presence, one student, Madelene, asked why I was not wearing a white shirt like all the other patriots. Realising that my duplicity had been discovered, I walked to the door. Albert, holding his umbrella like a weapon, prevented my escape:

> ALBERT: [Preventing my escape] *No you don't.*
>
> TEDDY: *Kill him.* [Lots of animation now from the group]
>
> PHIL: [Looking at Albert's gun] *I wouldn't advise that you use that.* [After a pause] *I have to inform you that this place will soon be surrounded. You will all be taken in as traitors to King George III* [Looks of disbelief]. *We have Molineux down at the courthouse.*
>
> MERYL: *I knew it!*
>
> PHIL: *He has confessed that he is a patriot. You have told me things here tonight that incriminate you all. You are all patriots. You are all traitors to King George III.*
>
> MERYL: [Fed up] *That's enough!* [To Albert] *Shoot him!!*
>
> [Frantic cries of 'Kill him! Kill him!' They are all standing]
>
> PHIL: *Don't be ridiculous. The soldiers will be outside shortly. You can't escape. You are disloyal and treacherous to King George III. You'll be punished. Each and everyone of you will be punished . . .*

The tension of the moment was experienced by all. Once the group's emotions were aroused I suspected that our decision-taking might assume greater urgency. Drama praxis has the ability to elevate emotional response within the protective medium of story. Although the group is working within a make-believe situation they are drawing on their own understanding of real-world behaviour as they negotiate a course of action. How does one deal with a troublemaker? When the patriots decided that they would kill the spy I confronted them with the implications of their decision. The patriots had decided to murder the host. What consequences might this stance have?

As you'll read in the transcript below, it was a demanding task for them to make a decision. They canvassed a number of possibilities: hiding in the ceiling, finding a secret doorway, climbing down the Liberty Tree, dressing up as a Tory, and shooting the soldiers. It was frustrating for them to select one. Each possibility had merits, so it was therefore a complex choice. Occasionally they would look my way for assistance, probably hoping that teacher would provide the correct answer; but the looks over time became less frequent. Perhaps they realised that there was no correct answer. Often in social studies it is questionable whether the teachers' suggestions are more authentic than the children's, since the teachers' solutions may have no better factual or analytic bases than those of the children being taught.

The group now encountered a number of options, each equally attractive. 'Intellectual development', Bruner suggests, 'is marked by an increasing capacity to deal with several alternatives simultaneously' (1966, p. 6). When Meryl hastily convened a vote as though this would automatically solve the problem, I hoped the group would become aware of the possible implications of their decision:

 MERYL: *All right so we'll climb out the Liberty Tree.*
PHIL: *So you leave the traitor's body there?*
TOM: *Yeah* [others agree]
PHIL: *You leave that bloodied Tory's body at the doorstep of this house?*
MERYL: *Yeah, and Teddy can put his sign* [which has the words, 'No Lobsterbacks'] *on it.*
PHIL: *Does everyone agree to that?* [Chorus of 'yes']
MERYL: *And with the sign on it.*
TOM: [Pleased] *An intimidation!*
PHIL: [Thoughtfully] *You then incriminate this house, William Molineux's house, as being a meeting place for the patriots?* [Pause. Long pause. They had not considered this] *Is that what you want to do?* [Deathly silence]

The dilemma the students were now in was powerful. If they escaped from the house and left the body behind they might put Molineux, a friend and respected fellow patriot, in greater danger than he already was. Immediate self-interest versus possible disloyalty appeared to be an issue here. Would they become traitors to Molineux if they escaped and left the body? What are the personal costs of loyalty?

In the ensuing silence, the group appeared to be constructing their own meaning of the events they had just witnessed, and particularly their own role in those events. Awareness, Donalson argues, typically develops when something gives us pause:

> *and when consequently, instead of just acting, we stop to consider the possibilities of acting which are before us. The claim is that we heighten our awareness of what is actual by considering what is possible. We are conscious of what we do to the extent that we are conscious of what we do not do – of what we might have done. The notion of choice is thus central.* (Donalson, 1978, p. 97)

Although the patriots now understood that they could not simply leave the body behind, they were still undecided about what to do. Meryl's journal entry following the above session reflected the group's uncertainty:

> *We had no choice we had to kill him or else we would have been captured and torchered by the torres [sic] . . . We had to think positive and make a plan fast . . . Some suggested that we take them on but god knows how many of them their are were only twelve . . .*

Such contemplative thought revealed genuine emotional commitment to the drama. 'If I had the choice to change and start the meeting again', Amara wrote, 'I wouldn't reveal the plot to that tori [*sic*] and wouldn't kill him, just capture him . . . and trade him for William.' The drama had raised fruitful insights into how decisions are made and the appropriateness of individual actions.

Being authentic

The drama praxis described above contains many of the characteristics of storydrama. Children work from a story, in this case sections from a children's book on the Boston Massacre, as a springboard for dramatic activity. Unlike story dramatisation, where students would act out the events of the Boston Massacre, storydrama requires students to improvise their own unscripted playtext in partnership with the teacher. The teacher develops an 'insider's view', and seeks to understand the children's perceptions of events while helping the group understand his/her own (Duckworth, 1987, p. 112).

In the Boston drama, students considered issues related to justice, commitment, and betrayal. They were required to hypothesise, clarify, reach decisions, exercise responsibility, and bear the consequences. In giving meaning to events rather than receiving meaning, students understand their role in constructing knowledge. Whereas telling a story may begin to create the possibilities of knowledge construction, working through story in action interrogates the authenticity of these possibilities.

When the group later compared their imagined enacted version of a historical encounter with the recorded one, they were surprised with the poetic licence we had taken. 'Our meeting was more exciting,' Nadia mused, 'there were more things happening.' Teddy agreed: 'It was more lively', he said. 'You can see what's going on and then make it up as you go along.' Simply reading about the event or being told about it would not help Teddy 'see what's going on'.

The students' reactions indicated that the experience of participating in the drama was an important one for them. As I reflected on their responses to our Molineux meeting, and about the nature of history and the value of drama, I was reminded of Dorothy Heathcote:

 I have struggled to perfect techniques which allow my classes oppor-tunities to stumble upon authenticity in their work and to be able both to experience and reflect upon their experience at the same time: simultaneously to understand their journey while being both the cause and the medium of the work. (Heathcote, 1980, p. 11)

While I was troubled that the students' identification with the patriots' cause was value-laden and that it might not have presented a fair representation of the soldiers' plight, I knew that our future work in drama would challenge these distortions. Drama praxis has the rich capacity of permitting students to confront their own behaviours in action and analyse such behaviours from a variety of perspectives. Yet most of all, drama praxis can enable students like

Meryl to wonder to themselves as they raise their own questions concerning their world and their relationship to it. And is not such wonderment to be strived for as educators help their students commit to the curriculum? In Chapter 4 we will consider the issues which educators need to take account of when designing curriculum committed to drama praxis.

Notes

1 See David Booth, ' "Imaginary gardens with real toads": reading and drama in education', *Theory into Practice*, **XXIV**, 3, pp. 193–198.
2 See David Booth (1987) pp. 60–74.
3 See David Hornbrook, *Education and Dramatic Art* (2nd edn) (London: Routledge, 1998).
4 See Aidan Chambers, *Tell Me: Children, Reading and Talk* (London: The Thimble Press, 1993).
5 All references to the children are through pseudonym.
6 See Willi Baum, 'The expedition', in D. Booth and Charles Lundy, *Improvisation* (Toronto: Harcourt Brace, 1985).
7 David Booth, in P. Taylor, *Pre-text and Storydrama* (Brisbane: National Association for Drama in Education, 1995).
8 Ibid.
9 See David Booth, 'Reflections of a shape shifter: searching for drama in the shadows', in J. Carey, J. Clark and T. Goode (eds) *Drama and the Making of Meanings* (Newcastle upon Tyne: National Drama Publications), pp. 15–28.
10 Ibid.
11 Maxine Greene, 'Art worlds in schools', in P. Abbs, *The Symbolic Order* (London: Falmer), p. 216.
12 All references to students are through pseudonyms. Phil is the teacher. Readers are referred to my book *Redcoats and Patriots: Reflective Practice in Drama and Social Studies* for further descriptions of this work (see Resources section at end of volume).

References

Barton, B. and Booth, D. (1990) *Stories in the Classroom*, Portsmouth, N.H.: Heinemann.

Booth, D. (1987) *Drama Words*, Toronto: Language Study Centre.

Booth, D. (1994) 'Entering the story cave', *The National Association for Drama In Education (NADIE) Journal*, **18**, 2, 67–77.

BRUNER, J. (1966) *Towards a Theory of Instruction*, Cambridge, Mass.: Harvard University Press.

COURTNEY, R. (1995) 'Preamble', in P. TAYLOR, *Pre-text and Storydrama*, Brisbane: National Association for Drama in Education.

DONALSON, M. (1978) *Children's Minds*, London: Tavistock.

DUCKWORTH, E. (1987) *'The Having of Wonderful Ideas' and Other Essays on Teaching and Learning*, New York: Teachers College Press.

GIROUX, H. (1988) *Teachers as Intellectuals*, Westport, Conn.: Bergin & Garvey.

GIROUX, H. and MCLAREN, P. (eds) (1993) *Between Borders: Pedagogy and the Politics of Cultural Studies*, New York: Routledge.

HEATHCOTE, D. (1980) 'From the particular to the universal', In K. ROBINSON (ed.) *Exploring Theatre and Education*, London: Heinemann, pp. 7–50.

HUME, K. and WELLS, G. (1999) 'Making lives meaningful: extending perspectives through role-play', in B. J. WAGNER (ed.) *Building Moral Communities through Educational Drama*, Stamford, Conn.: Ablex, pp. 63–87.

HUNKINS, F. (1969) 'The questions asked: effectiveness of inquiry techniques in elementary school social studies', in J. JAROLIMEK and H. M. WALSH (eds) *Readings for Social Studies in Elementary Education*, Toronto: Macmillan, pp. 186–195.

MCLAREN, P. (1989) *Life in Schools*, New York: Longman.

PHELAN, M. K. (1976) *The Story of the Boston Massacre*, New York: Thomas Crowell.

SHAUGHNESSY, J. M. and HALADYNA, T. M. (1985) 'Research on student attitude toward social studies', *Social Education*, **49**, 8, pp. 692–695.

STEVENS, R. (1912) 'The question as a measure of efficiency in instruction', *Teachers College Contributions to Education*, **48**.

WELLS, G. (1986) *The Meaning Makers: Children Learning Language and Using Language to Learn*, Portsmouth, N.H.: Heinemann.

Chapter 4

Designing drama curriculum

We are now faced with the problem of how to design curriculum in drama, given the ephemeral and transitory nature of its praxis. As the previous chapters have identified, the spontaneous and improvisational nature of drama praxis makes it difficult to pinpoint in functional quantitative terms what the attainment targets are. It is perhaps not surprising that some educators have tried to fit the dynamic and evolving drama curriculum into an outcome-oriented programme, with the outcomes essentially being those extrinsic skills and attitudes which can be observed and measured, rather the intrinsic changes which happen inside humans when they experience a work of art. The examples of drama praxis given to date (e.g., the wolf drama, the seal-wife, the invaders, and the patriots) are characterised by their exploration of values and attitudes, and how such can be interrogated and transformed. Such praxis does not lend itself easily to numerical attainment.

The last two decades of the twentieth century witnessed incredible curriculum activity in the arena of international arts education. Drama educators formed partnerships with their arts counterparts in dance, media, music and visual art. If the arts were to survive as a curriculum entity in schools, there was a political imperative for the arts to join forces and to present a united front. When designing curriculum in drama, the argument was put that educators need to be conscious of the skills or competencies which the arts present as a generic offering.

The National Coalition of Arts Education Organizations in the US was not alone in its endeavour to lobby for standards in arts education. Similar activity had been happening in the UK (even though in England, dance and drama are not part of the core arts curriculum). In Australia, during the last two decades of the millennium, much attention and government money was directed to the preparation of a comprehensive arts curriculum. Like the US Arts Coalition, Australian educational leaders identified levels of achievement in arts education by isolating learning stages. As well, they agreed upon the principles and outcomes which should inform a school's arts programme. Although education is a state responsibility in Australia, the national statements and profiles, as they became known, hold considerable currency in local curriculum planning.

Such negotiations required considerable goodwill from all parties, often demanding the ability to compromise and, if necessary, acquiesce on matters of disagreement. I sympathise with Hope's reflection in an issue of *Arts Education Policy Review* that achieving consensus on national standards in arts education can be an 'intense' experience and can generate exhausting emotional debates.[1] Australian arts education experienced similar frustrations and joys. These responses were inevitable given the intellectual debate associated when faced with numerous, often competing perspectives. While drama educators, for example, believed in the power of their artform to change and influence human activity, the reality was that music and visual art were the mainstays of the arts curriculum. The added dimension of funding from the Australian Federal Government placed these discussions in the public domain. Public accountability laced nationwide attempts at curriculum consensus with added tension.

For all of the good conversation that can occur when educators come together to prepare standards and attainment, I am concerned that published curriculum packages can shift the onus of professional responsibility from the teachers in schools to the package. While I understand the importance of arts educators networking on a national and international level, and the economic and political realities of promoting the field of arts education, there seems to me to be some very serious traps in this process that might dangerously snare arts educators and thereby do irrevocable harm to their work.

In this chapter, I plan to tease out these concerns by isolating the unique features of an arts education and to suggest how the successful implementation of an arts programme depends on the ongoing reflective practice of teachers. I intend to reveal how comprehensive attempts at national standards, statements, or profiles in the arts, no matter how soundly rationalised, may unwittingly undermine the work of the practising educator. I conclude with a discussion on how the existentialist nature of drama praxis requires educators to be sensitive to their own ability to read the immediate context and to develop their own skills of reflective praxis.

What is an arts education?

When I was teaching creative drama in a New York elementary school last century, I would not have described myself as an arts educator. Drama or theatre would have been the response if somebody asked what I taught. Likewise, when I was directing school plays in an Australian high school I did not liken my practice to arts teaching. Again, if asked about my position, I would have said that I taught drama. While I expect that if I was working back in those settings and with similar conditions today I would use the same words, I anticipate there would be a significant elaboration: arts educator.

No doubt in the current climate, music, dance and visual arts teachers also have looked beyond their immediate discipline when describing their field. 'I work in the arts', or, 'I belong to an arts faculty' are now the familiar retorts of such specialists. Why is it that 'arts educator' has crept into the vernacular of the music, dance, theatre or visual arts specialist? How is it that just a few years ago these specialists would rarely have asserted, in the first instance, that their work fell within arts education?

If the experiences of Australia, Canada, England and the US are an indication of global trends, political imperatives have driven arts specialists to align in a manner previously not considered. In Australia, for example, the arts were identified by a governmental body as one of eight key learning areas which all children should have access to. National consultation promoted the view that the arts consisted of five key strands: dance, drama, media, music and visual arts (the latter incorporating art, craft and design).[2] Unlike the England situation where only visual art and music were promoted as foundation subjects in the national curriculum, Australia did not prioritise one artform over another. Although an Australian music professor expressed alarm at such equity between the artforms, and feared the 'down-grading of the existing status of music in general education',[3] there was widespread agreement that the five arts strands redressed the historical imbalance of promoting music and art as central to an arts education.

In the US, the lobbying of the Consortium of National Arts Education Associations led to the arts having a heightened profile and being included in national education goals.[4] It may be useful to explore the emphases on the arts in Australia and the US, as a starting point for a discussion on curriculum planning.

Of interest are the significant differences in the terminology employed within the Australian and US context. Whereas Australia lists five arts *strands*, the US highlights the four arts *disciplines* as being:

- Dance
- Music (including opera and musical theatre)
- Theatre (including theatrical performance, film, and electronic media)
- Visual Arts (including traditional fine arts, design and communication arts, the media arts, the environmental and architectural arts, folk arts, and crafts)[5]

Not only does the term 'discipline' suggest an intellectual content, it also implies a separate and coherent identity. From my observations, US arts educators have not been bashful about employing terms such as 'discipline', 'content', 'standards' in their curriculum statements. Other nations, such as Australia where progressivist notions have permeated thinking in arts education for some time, have emphasised methodological concerns and teaching contexts. This view is confirmed when the US standards state that students should be able to communicate in the four arts disciplines and to be proficient in at least one art form. Although the Australian documents referred to level learning outcomes they do not specifically claim 'what students should know and be able to do in the arts'.

The expression 'Areas of Competence' is not used in the Australian document. The US arts standards construe competence in three ways:

- Creating and Performing (which refers to arts-making processes)
- Perceiving and Analysing (the ability to discriminate and value)

■ Understanding Cultural and Historical Contexts (the knowledge of criticism and history)

Although the Australian arts statements and profiles employ a similar construction, referred to as 'strand organisers', rather than express 'areas of competence' these 'describe key learning areas within the five strands'. The Australian strand organisers are:

■ Creating, making and presenting
■ Arts Criticism and Aesthetics
■ Past and Present Contexts

There is a differentiation of 'making' from 'creating' in the Australian documents, whereas both are seen as part of the same competency in the US. Also, Australian visual arts educators, unlike those in the other arts strands, could not agree that standards or level outcomes could be discretely listed under presenting. 'Students experience the visual arts by learning to be makers and creators, critics and theorists', argues the National Statement on the Arts for Australian Schools. 'To a lesser extent,' it states, 'they also present their work for others to see and enjoy.'[6] In the US document the three areas of competence apply, without exception, to the four arts disciplines.

Despite the differences in terminology and construction of the Australian and US documents they share a lot in common. Both have been driven by a political imperative. The arts, it seems, have to be presented in utilitarian ways if they are going to play a central role in the national agenda. Children have to be seen to benefit from the arts if the arts are to be included in school programmes. Standards, outcomes, proficiencies are being articulated in the arts as they have been for other learning areas. The arts, we are informed, are about communication systems; they involve literacy skills, they express human achievement and understanding. 'The arts are powerful economic forces as well,' argues the US National Standards, 'from fashion, to the creativity and design that go into every manufactured product, to architecture, to the performance and entertainment arts that have grown into multi-billion dollar industries.'[7]

When politicians adopt the rhetoric so often used in these documents there is a sense that curriculum leaders are impacting on the national agenda. 'It is not enough for students to acquire knowledge and skills in a set of defined subjects', argued an Ontario Minister for Education in Canada last century. Emphasising the unique contribution of the arts, he maintained:

 They must also learn about the connections and relationships between subjects, and among ideas, people and events. Study of the arts, especially of the concepts of pattern and form, can provide students with strong critical tools for learning and communicating in all areas of life.[8]

The arts can be justified on a variety of different levels for an all-encompassing range of purposes, and indeed are.

I do not want to undermine the importance of ministerial statements like that expressed above, or the various rationales provided in curriculum documents to support the arts; but an irony exists in these claims, an irony that possibly ignores the reality of arts practices in schools. Rarely, does it seem to me, do arts teachers conceive of themselves and their work in the manner which the documents espouse. Music, theatre, visual art and dance teachers, or however one distinguishes arts educators, have not developed a sense of shared competencies or developed a united vision. While curriculum documents may lead to such unity and camaraderie I am not convinced that arts specialists naturally gravitate in this manner.

Historically, for instance, theatre/drama teachers have had little to communicate to their visual arts colleagues, and vice versa. In visual arts where classroom work has been characterised by solitary, even anti-social, endeavour, theatre is distinguished by its small and whole group co-operative interaction. There could not be a more brutal distinction of learning processes from one artform to the next. In my experience, the few times I worked with the visual art specialist or music teacher was when I was directing a school play or musical. At best, these services were solicited to support a specialist endeavour rather than lead to an informed understanding of an arts education. At worst, they were merely decorative. In the past, I cannot recall a conversation I have had with music and art colleagues in an elementary, middle- or high-school about the constitution of an arts education, and certainly no discussion on the formulation of an arts curriculum comes to mind.

Now, perhaps my experiences are not representative of the rich and dynamic interaction that occurs within arts departments across

Australian, British, Canadian and US education faculties today; but, if the collections of papers on arts education assembled by the National Society for the Study of Education (US) and Deakin University Press (Australia) are any indication, there is little dialogue occurring among art specialists at the grass-roots level. The ideas appear to be generated at a level beyond the school. Furthermore, the authors of the articles contained within these collections are typically full-time employees of university faculties who promulgate theories to be adopted in settings they do not work in.[9] Even the arts specialists in the academy do not appear to be engaged in ongoing and sustained dialogue with their colleagues, and one assumes that they have more time to engage in such banter than the elementary school teacher burdened with five, sometimes six, hours of daily teaching.

Why is it that the voices of teachers do not dominate the design of the curriculum documents? Why is it that of the thirty-five names listed as committee members of the National K-12 Standards for Arts Education in the US only three (two high-school teachers and one principal of an elementary school) could be considered direct representatives of the predominant sites where these standards will be achieved?

While I am sensitive to Hope's concern that if we are too critical of these statements and raise too many fears with them we may become immune to their inherent value:

 As history has shown, the lack of standards can also be harmful. Let us also be wise enough not to promote the standards as a panacea but rather as a basic tool for fashioning the future that must be supported by the development of new tools and by the wise use of tools we already have.[10]

I cannot help but remind him of his words, 'Integrity involves being honest about what the standards can and cannot do.'[11] I find it interesting, for example, that in Australia $60.5 million (Australian dollars) was set aside some years back by the Federal Government to facilitate teachers' use of the curriculum statements and profiles when those very teachers had minimal input into the design and content of those documents. In other words, the published curriculum framework was not the focus of scrutiny but the teachers' delivery of it.

In raising these concerns I am not questioning the intentions of the many devoted arts educators in Australia and the United States who invested the time preparing these materials, often under extremely tight deadlines, but rather I am alerting policy-makers to substantial gaps in arts curricula when they do not include the experiences of school teachers when *generating* programme content and learning outcomes.

Relating reflective practice to arts education

Although political expediencies are often the driving forces behind nationwide curriculum initiatives, these can conflict with the professional integrity of the arts educator. When the voluntary standards for K-12 arts education arrived in US schools, and as the Australian arts statements and profiles informed the practice of teachers, the professional development of educators, inevitably, takes place in relation to these documents.

It can be difficult for educators to generate their own standards, statements and profiles in light of the glossy and impressively produced publications. There was a risk that arts educators will not believe in their own capacities to generate standards, statements and profiles, but will perform in relation to others. Undoubtedly those who worked on and developed these documents gained enormously from the project. Their own professional in-servicing challenged them to consider the nature of an arts education and how it should be constructed. Samuel Hope's description of one aspect of the process which the 'relatively small but extremely dedicated' US writers experienced is informative. When describing how the group decided upon content statements in the standards development process, he states:

> it became more and more clear that knowledgeable people could agree on content. There is a fundamental body of knowledge and skills for each of the art disciplines. It became equally clear that there was much less agreement on how this content should be packaged or on the methodologies, experiences, resources, and curriculum sequences needed to teach it. The joyous result, however, was that the drafters began to discover an important fundamental principle: agreement on content and disagreement on packaging and delivery

systems represents strength rather than weakness. Those involved in the project arrived at substance over form and lived to tell the tale.[12]

I envy the debate that Hope experienced with his colleagues at moments like those characterised above. Yet, I fear that only those who were present can be the beneficiaries of this process. Unfortunately, only a few arts educators are privileged to participate in such rich and illuminating discussions.

Even more frustrating is that politically induced curricula can distort the fabric of what an education in the arts disciplines has historically entailed. Artists search for an appropriate form to express content. They create moments which are constantly transformed in the artist's and spectator's mind. Each artwork provokes questions in its attempt to raise some light or express a truth about the world. The arts, if anything, are non-conventional language systems that require their own unique modes of comprehension.

By trying 'to ensure parity with the other K-12 disciplines'[13] the integrity of the arts may falter. Rather than raise questions, curriculum packages tend to shut inquiry down, or, at best, present inquiry within restrictive parameters. While I do not totally despair I do worry that the teacher's own reflective practice does not seem to be a priority in these documents. If teachers can be encouraged to ask questions like, How can I be a more effective arts teacher? When do my students seem to be engaged in arts education? What leads to arresting artistic experiences with a particular group?, rather than ask, What content standard am I working on today? Which competencies must I teach? How will I achieve a level four outcome?, I am confident that arts education classrooms will avoid dreary and lifeless pedagogical practices. Reflective practice can be the agent that will command teachers and students to explore the fabric of classroom life, assess its vital elements, and enable them to respond to perceived strengths and weaknesses with authoritative efficacy.

The case for reflective practice

 So many of us today confine ourselves to right angles. We function in the narrowest of specialties; we lead one-dimensional lives. We accommodate ourselves so easily to the demands of the technological

society – to time schedules, charts, programs, techniques – that we lose touch with our streams of consciousness, our inner time.[14]

It seems appropriate to begin this section with a quotation from Maxine Greene, the illuminating American educator, historian and philosopher. Greene has devoted much of her professional career to promoting what she describes as wideawakeness, an alert state of consciousness where individuals reflect on the world and the role they play in it. Greene's concern is that teachers reluctantly become strangers to their own practice. Professional growth, she asserts, is located in teachers' ability to revisit their work with renewed eyes and possibly transform themselves through a deliberate and critical self-examination of their own fallible pedagogy.

It is perhaps no surprise to learn of Greene's indebtness to John Dewey and his championing of the individual's capacity to remind oneself to reconsider, to stop, pause, meditate, and contemplate an issue or phenomenon in a different way and thereby provoke an enlightened perspective. There is clearly a contradiction between raising teacher consciousness and delivering externally developed standards and profiles. Inevitably, the odds are against teachers assuming the stance of knowledgeable practitioners capable of reflective thought and who can assume responsibility for their own professional development when others, outside their classroom, have been charged with this responsibility.

But common sense dictates that if teachers depend on others to do their thinking for them they inevitably will become automatons in their own classrooms. Clar Doyle, in a book on the role of critical pedagogy in the drama classroom,[15] claims that education is not a neutral process and cannot be denuded of the social, human, and historical elements that make up the process of teaching. Educators, he suggests, have not always been willing to account for their own and their students' 'socially determined taste, prior knowledge, language forms, abilities and modes of knowing'.[16] Both Doyle and Greene remind us that each classroom is affected by its own cultural milieu. Students and their teachers bring to the educational event an array of cultural and particular ethnic biases.

Teachers, then, need to activate their own ability to think, assess and re-assess within their own school communities. Just as the playwright and drama critic, Bertolt Brecht, was concerned with developing techniques to distance the spectator from the dramatic action if the play was to confront the audience to consider the truths of the world, arts educators need to find similar distancing strategies to examine their praxis. Clearly, the reflective practitioner is one such approach.

The term 'reflective practitioner' has been widely promoted in the field of architectural design by Donald Schön.[17] It is sometimes referred to as teacher-research, critical pedagogy or action research, although each labelling has its own histories and emphases. Reflective practitioners empower themselves to contemplate critically some aspect of their own teaching and learning processes. They tend to be suspicious of published curriculum documents that have not been grounded in and powered by actual classroom experiences. Reflective practitioners are interested in searching for their own themes on classroom inquiry which directly inform their immediate and ongoing praxis.

I can identify nine characteristics of reflective practitioners. Readers will note an overlap here with many of the principles of drama praxis.

Reflective practitioners are:

1 Critical thinkers
Rather than accepting curriculum programmes at face value reflective practitioners are sensitive to the historical and political contexts which led to their publication.

2 Producers of knowledge
Reflective practitioners are suspicious about consuming the values, attitudes, and ideas of others. They recognise that the informed classroom environment demands the active production of relevant material.

3 Risk takers
Following the crowd can be easier than standing alone. Reflective practitioners recognise the difficulties in activating their classrooms as sites of critical inquiry when typically the authorities are believed to exist outside the classroom.

4 Theory generators

Based on direct observation of practice, reflective practitioners develop their own informed theories on teaching and learning. These theories are constantly transformed in practice.

5 Prepared to fail

Often when attempting a new approach or responding to immediate demands we are liable to error. Reflective practitioners understand that success can come through perceived failure.

6 Open-minded and flexible

Reflective practitioners try to develop multi-perspectives on a particular classroom event. They must be sensitive to different voices and capable of re-thinking cherished ideas.

7 Collaborative

Reflective practitioners recognise that they do not work alone. They engage their students, their colleagues, and the wider school community in their endeavour to create rich learning centres.

8 Revising teaching and learning procedures

The cultural capital of each classroom is different. Reflective practitioners are aware that strategies and content appropriate in one setting may not be appropriate in another.

9 Story-makers and story-listeners

Reflective practitioners listen and respond to their own stories and those of their students. Classrooms become sites for story-telling, story-responding and story-creating.

To be an arts educator is to be a reflective practitioner. Both give birth to ideas; both search for a medium to express and honour their vision. Artists, like reflective practitioners:

> are for disclosing the extraordinary in the ordinary. They are for transfiguring the commonplace, as they embody their perceptions and feelings and understandings in a range of languages, in formed substance of many kinds. They are for affirming the work of imagination – the cognitive capacity that summons up the 'as if', the possible, the what is not and yet what might be. They are for doing all this in such a way as to enable those who open themselves to what they create to

see more, to hear more, to feel more, to attend to more facets of the experienced world.[18]

Empowering teachers as artists: balancing *What is happening now?* with *What is happening next?*

To have an experience of art, we need to project ourselves into the artwork, we need to encounter it, and allow it to speak to us. I am reminded how in my own life the most powerful encounters I have had with arts are those where I have had an internal conversation between the work and myself.

For some time now I've been fascinated with how the arts, particularly the arts in schools, provide us with opportunities to express who we are and what we hope to become. This observation became very clear some years back when I was employed as a seventh-grade teacher in Chinatown, New York. The students, 95 per cent being from Asian background, loved to draw. Whenever they had free time they would pull out their drawing pads and begin to sketch. These pictures might be faithful realistic portraits of friends in the class, or bright colourful renderings of comic strip characters. It seemed that drawing was helping them to construct their own understanding of various phenomena.

The content of the curriculum became the stimulus for much of their artwork. If we were reading aloud a popular children's text, *The Hobbit* for instance, my kids would draw their version of characters or scenes from the book. If we were studying various indigenous folktales or mythologies, the students, on their own initiative, would render these stories through picture in their workbooks. They were passionate about drawing, and when it was our grade's turn, the seventh grade's responsibility, to prepare the bulletin boards in the corridors, my kids would take the theme, whatever it was – Halloween, Thanksgiving, the Chinese New Year – and attend to the task with precision and detail.

I felt that my own lack of proficiency in the visual arts let my seventh-graders down, but when I knew that I was never going to be as skilled as they were in drawing, I released myself from the burden of being the authority figure, and cast myself into the role of the one who supports and encourages their interest. I've often thought that teachers work most effectively when they release themselves to the moment, when they can recognise the context in which they work, and allow the circumstances of their work environment to shape what is possible and what is not possible.

I know that curriculum standards and frameworks can be very helpful because they provide us with some idea of the boundaries, or the playing field in which we work. It is important that students not only learn how to create, perform, critique and reflect in the arts, but that they also understand how the arts contribute to cultural advancement. One advantage of standards is that they provide us with benchmarks, and can ensure that the children are not being denied access to a full range of competencies in the arts.

However, as I've discussed, standards can also have the unfortunate result that they can reduce the curriculum to a series of outputs. Rather than teachers being arrested by the moment, by What is happening now?, they are driven by What is happening next? We all can recognise a teacher who asks that question, What is happening next? They move through the curriculum as if it were a discrete body of information which needs to be digested by the children. They are governed by endpoints, the end of the chapter, the final production, the test, and emphasise the product over the process.

If such teachers were to ask themselves a different kind of question – rather than what is happening next?, what is happening now? – they would be challenged to investigate the moment, to look closely at what happens to children when they are caught up in the here and now. But unfortunately schooling seems to work against the here and now, being more interested in having students perform pre-ordained tasks and achieving prescribed attainment levels.

If students are going to learn anything from their encounters with good artworks, they need to develop a conversation with them. They must have an experience of an artwork if they are to engage with it. And if we can provide students with satisfying arts experiences they will begin, hopefully, to understand how the arts operate as live encounters between the artist and the audience.

Just as artists represent their own vision of their world, and are drawn to the question What is happening in my world now?, so too are the observers of the artwork coming to an understanding of the world as they encounter the artists' work. The spectator becomes a spect-actor, who actively works to construct meaning. Spectators, or spect-actors, are always asking the question What is happening now? as they begin to dialogue with the artwork.[19]

As arts educators we must not lose sight of the power of the artform to transform, to move and shift us. I am thinking here of the existential experience, the lived moment, the encounter between what is created and what is perceived. This poses some real dilemmas for teachers. In Chapter 3 readers were introduced to my seventh-graders, and how I was required to teach them the social studies curriculum. I noticed that the children's textbook was focused on American history. A colleague at the school told me that as long as the students were studying the Civil War by June I would have done a good job. As most of my teaching work had been in drama and language arts I thought I was grossly under-prepared to teach this subject. However, in my preparation I read somewhere that at the heart of good teaching in social studies was to shift the emphasis from the mastery of information to an emphasis of having students struggle with the contradictions. Rather than seeing my role as one who taught American history, I should enable students to grapple with difficult and opposing ideas. I liked that idea of having the kids struggle with the contradictions. I was reminded that this struggle is at the centre of artistic activity.

Art at its most effective presents conflicting, ambiguous and often disturbing images; the least effective uses of art, in my view, are those which instruct or which are wholly didactic. Likewise, good social studies teaching, I was to learn, was not just about facts and information, but about grappling with concepts. Wow! Social studies was not about teaching a truth contained within a textbook but having students formulate their own truths, and understanding that truths can be contradictory, ambiguous, multiple and shifting.

And isn't this idea the guiding philosophy of artists: that truths are multiple and shifting?

Shifting truths

At the centre of good arts education practice, it seems to me, is giving permission for teachers to ask that question, What is happening now? I remember Meryl from my seventh-grade class;

readers met her in Chapter 3. She was of Spanish origins, one of the few non-Asian students in the group. I asked her once to describe what a typical social studies class entailed for her. 'We would be reading the book', she said, a reference to this huge 800-page textbook called *The Challenge of the World*.[20] 'We would be talking about climate, the world, it really wouldn't be all that interesting.'

'And what kinds of task would you do in social studies?' I asked.

'Oh, we would answer questions from the book. She would ask us questions' ('she' being her previous teacher) 'and we would take down notes in our workbooks, then we would do a chapter test and that's really it.'

What an uninspired list of activities I thought. When I spoke with other students in Meryl's class, they would repeat the kinds of things she said. 'We would take notes from the board, we would do tests, and then do the next chapter.'

I was surprised that these students were not being more actively engaged in their curriculum. The most interactive form of encounter appeared to be a teacher-led discussion where the answers were either right or wrong. There was no talk of small group work, no talk of creative projects; there was certainly no mention of drama activity. Social studies in this classroom seemed governed by recycling the information in the book, and the teacher checking that this recycling had been done effectively. I later discovered though that this view of social studies is quite a common one in schools.

Given the passive and sedentary role that these students had been cast in, I knew that my work was going to be cut out for me to transform this negative disposition they had towards social studies. These children were twelve and thirteen years old, and had already developed a strong dislike to an area of the curriculum which, to my mind, should have been filled with the excitement of discovery, the desire to probe. I was reminded by those words I had read, that social studies education is about helping students struggle with the contradictions, so I was comforted by the connection here to drama praxis, an artform which is built around placing people in circumstances of discomfort, positions where they are out of sorts with the world.

Good drama praxis in education aims to devise roles and situations which explore the human condition – not as a way of answering the problems of the world, but to help develop a perspective on the world and to understand or at least struggle with the perspectives of others as we all move to a sense of social justice and equity.

I knew that I had at my hands a powerful artistic modality in drama which I could slowly introduce in my social studies classroom, introduce in a way that the students would be protected and supported. As I described in Chapter 3, drama praxis helped the students commit to the curriculum, it provided an immediate perspective on the events. The praxis enabled them to struggle with the contradictions of being an American patriot who had to work through a dilemma; it required them to interpret the lives of people under stress, and it challenged them to reconstruct a portrait of the times being studied.

Yes, the artform was being used to teach the curriculum, if you like, but this kind of method justification does not really do the arts justice. The arts help to create a curriculum, they shouldn't be seen as secondary or extra-curricula. The arts enable students to commit, and they do so by providing participants (teachers and students) with the chance to reflect on themselves and their world. In other words, they ask that question: What is happening to me now?

Conclusion: curriculum as reflective practice

The most effective educators are able to reflect on the kind of teachers they are and the possible teachers they can become. When teachers and their students begin to look at themselves as they commit to curriculum, they are reflecting on the question, What is happening to me now?

Reflection, though, requires distance. As teachers and students gain distance they can begin to see how the work operates. They are better able to reflect on the question, What is happening to me now? As teachers and student gain distance, they, like artists, can appraise the created work. Good educators then, like good artists, are able to reflect upon and demonstrate their understanding of the world and their place in that world.

I am not sure whether the division between artist and educator is entirely helpful, because to my mind the best educators in drama praxis are working as artists, as indeed the best artists are working as educators. Arts works operate as reflective events. We can all think of examples where a performance, an exhibition, a recital, has unnerved us, leaving us with a slight sense of unease, an uncomfortable yet necessary disturbance; an artistic event that has generated more questions than it answers. An event from my own experience might help clarify my thinking here.

When I saw a performance of the Vineyard Theatre's production of Paula Vogel's play, *How I Learned to Drive* in Manhattan, I was reminded of the integral connection between art and education. In Vogel's play, the unsettling questions focused on sexual awakening. The play raises unnerving issues about child sexual abuse, and, the audience's, perhaps unknown, complicity in such events. The play focuses on Li'l Bit, a woman who, we are told, ages 'forty something' to eleven years old. The play is a series of reflections on Li'l Bit's life, and as her story unfolds, and as we witness the relationship which is developing between her and her Uncle Peck, our response is not simply one of outrage but of uncertainty as we struggle with the complex portraits of the characters' lives.

How I Learned to Drive is told, in part, through the eyes of a Greek Chorus, a device I'm sure Vogel selected so that the audience could be further distanced from the events in order to understand them more fully. The Greek Chorus assumes various roles and situations that surround Li'l Bit and Uncle Peck. And as the Chorus demonstrate their various parts, we project our own lives into those displayed before us, seeing our own frailties, passions, hopes and dreams.

Towards the end of the play, one Greek Chorus member assumes the character of Aunt Mary, Uncle Peck's wife. Aunt Mary is a complex woman. She loves her husband, knows that he has a personality which is, for want of a better term, on the edge. At the same time she is a confused woman, who looks for scapegoats and deflects responsibility from herself and Peck on to others.

> *My husband was such a good man – is. Is such a good man. Every night, he does the dishes. The second he comes home, he's taking out the garbage, or doing yard work, lifting the heavy things I can't.*

Everyone in the neighbourhood borrows Peck – it's true – women with husbands of their own, men who don't have Peck's abilities . . .

I know he has troubles. And we don't talk about them. I wonder sometimes what happened to him during the war. The men who fought World War II didn't have 'rap sessions' to talk about their feelings . . . I know he's having a bad spell because he comes looking for me in the house, and just hangs around me until it passes. And I keep my banter light – I discuss a new recipe, or sales, or gossip – because I think domesticity can be balm for men when they're lost. We sit in the house and listen to the peace of the clock ticking in his well-ordered living room, until it passes.

[Sharply] I'm not a fool. I know what's going on. I wish you could feel how hard Peck fights against it – he's swimming against the tide, and what he needs is to see me on the shore, believing in him, knowing he won't go under, he won't give up –

And I want to say this about my niece. She's a sly one, that one is. She knows exactly what she's doing; she's twisted Peck around her little finger and thinks it's all a big secret. Yet another one who's borrowing my husband until it doesn't suit her anymore.

Well. I'm counting the days until she goes away to school. And she manipulates someone else. And then he'll come back again, and sit in the kitchen while I bake, or beside me on the sofa when I sew in the evenings. I'm a very patient woman. But I'd like my husband back.

I'm counting the days.   (Vogel, 1998, pp. 66–67)

And when she finished with those words, 'I'm counting the days', I reflected on the kind of compromises that woman has made, and the costs of such compromises on herself and those around her. I wondered to what extent I too close myself off to reality, ignoring the pain, the inhumanity and suffering that surrounds me. How often do I blame the Li'l Bits of this world for others' failings? Vogel unnerves us because we have to project ourselves into the work if it is to reach us. And maybe if it is to reach us fully we need to locate aspects of Aunt Mary, of Li'l Bit and maybe even of Uncle Peck that exist in all of us.

If by the word 'educate' we mean there is a need to help others search, to draw them out, to raise the level of consciousness and insight, to question and probe, *How I Learned to Drive* fulfils the criterion of an educative work. But it too is an artwork, a subtly rendered work, which operates through the imagination, through a metaphor if you like, that permits contemplative and reflective thought.

For teachers 'though' to ask that question, What is happening to me now?, when they are evaluated on What is happening next?, is a difficult challenge. But at the end of the day it is the teacher who is implementing the curriculum in his or her classroom in partnership with the students, the school community, the Boards of Education and other vested interest groups. Ultimately, if teachers are to find ways of helping students commit to the curriculum, then they need to manage their work in partnership with these vested interests. How to manage these partnerships is the focus of chapter six. In the next chapter we consider the changing conceptualisations of drama curriculum.

Notes

1 Samuel Hope, 'An open letter on standards', *Arts Education Policy Review* (September/October 1993), pp. 36–39.
2 The Australian Arts Statements and Profiles are published by the Curriculum Corporation. Information concerning these documents should be directed to: Curriculum Corporation, P.O. Box 177, Carlton South, Victoria 3053, Australia. Telephone: 61 3 9207 9600.
3 Robin S. Stevens, 'Music education in Australia', in E. Errington, *Arts Education: Beliefs, Practices and Possibilities* (Victoria, Australia: Deakin University Press, 1993), p. 59.
4 Samuel Hope's article is an excellent reference on the history and development of the national standards project in arts education.
5 Consortium of National Arts Education Associations (Draft, 1993) *National Standards for Education in the Arts: What Every Young American Should Know and Be Able to Do in the Arts*: Preface, p. v.
6 See p. 24 of the *National Statement on the Arts for Australian Schools*.
7 *National Standards for the Arts*, p. vii.
8 Cooke, in P. Taylor (1994) 'Obstacles to arts education', *The Arts Paper*, **5**, 1, pp. 1–4.
9 Two volumes of papers on arts education have been published in Australia and the US. Readers are directed to: National Society for the Study of Education, *The Arts, Education and Aesthetic Knowing* (Chicago, Ill.: National Society for the Study of Education, 1992), and

Errington, E. (ed.) *Arts Education: Beliefs, Practices and Possibilities* (Victoria, Australia: Deakin University Press, 1992).

10 Hope, op. cit., p. 38.

11 Ibid.

12 Ibid., p. 37.

13 Ibid., p. 39.

14 See Maxine Greene, *Landscapes of Learning* (New York: Teachers College Press, 1978), pp. 198–199.

15 Clar Doyle, *Raising Curtains on Education: Drama as a Site for Critical Pedagogy* (Westport, Conn.: Bergin & Garvey, 1993).

16 Ibid., p. 83.

17 Donald Schön, *The Reflective Practitioner* (New York: Basic Books, 1983).

18 Maxine Greene, 'Art worlds in schools', in Peter Abbs, *The Symbolic Order* (London: Falmer Press, 1989), p. 216.

19 I am indebted to Augusto Boal, the Brazilian theatre educator, for this term, spect-actor. See Resources section at end of volume.

20 Readers are referred to my text *Redcoats and Patriots: Reflective Practice in Drama and Social Studies* (Portsmouth, N.H.: Heinemann, 1998) for a more detailed account of this class.

Reference

Vogel, P. (1998) *The Mammary Plays*, New York: Theatre Communications Group.

Chapter 5

Historical perspectives on drama praxis

The past century witnessed a long and established tradition of presenting schoolchildren with opportunities to engage in dramatic playing activities. These activities, which have operated under a variety of different titles including improvisation, enactment, drama, theatre sports, youth theatre, role-playing, storydrama and process drama, to name a few, achieved a birthing of popularity during the so-called child-progressive era of the late 1960s and 1970s. During this period, movements like those launched in Dartmouth (Dixon, 1967), and the research of Vygotsky (1978), Moffett (1968), Britton (1971) and Bruner (1979), supported the interest in child play and its place in children's learning. In recent times, the investigative work of Wagner (1998) in drama and language development, of Manley and O'Neill (1995) in drama and multicultural education, and of Winston (1998) and Wagner (1999a) in drama and moral education, has helped us understand the far-ranging potential of drama praxis as a programmed curriculum offering.

However, for all the popularity in drama which led to the formation of professional organisations across the world, such as Drama Australia, an organisation which now totals 2,000 members, making it one of the largest associations in the world dedicated to classroom drama, there seemed to be a belief, primarily expressed by public authorities, that drama was as an extra, an option, or an addendum to mainstream education (Hughes, 1988). As drama had been located solely within the domain of educating feelings and emotions it was seen in opposition to work and intellect. In lean times and when the economic rationalist rules, subjects which aren't construed as central to mainstream learning are lopped from the timetable. Drama's uncompromising connection to emotion, to play, and to feelings, resulted in it gradually being eviscerated from school programmes. The great expansion in the 1960s and 1970s was being usurped by a drive for accountability. Drama, notably in England, and to a lesser extent Australia, was having difficulty advocating a convincing case for continuing curriculum inclusion.

Where the 1980s and 1990s were characterised by a downsizing in drama departments, no more evident than at Melbourne State College, now The University of Melbourne, which decreased its staffing from twelve full-time academic staff in 1977 to its current 'skeleton part-time staff member' (O'Brien and Dopierala, 1994: p. 26), there are clear signs that a renewal in drama praxis is now taking place, especially in Australia, England, and in parts of the USA. While the picture in Canada appears more sketchy, in other parts of the world not only does there appear to be a growing number of books being published on drama praxis, and more journals dedicated to its work, it seems that mistakes made have been learnt and that a broader conception of drama praxis has been framed.

While attempts to secure drama in national curriculum initiatives provided a political imperative to this redevelopment, there are numerous indications that drama is assuming a more dominant position within school programmes. In Australia, for example, the evidence that drama has begun to reassume a profile is convincing. This profile is evident through the growing numbers of students enrolled in senior drama programmes, through the increasing numbers of teachers exiting from universities with majors in drama, through the large number of teacher-researchers publishing and conference presenting, and through the increasing cohort of masters and doctoral research students. As well, there is recognition that teachers themselves have considerable autonomy to implement drama praxis in their own classrooms. It is also worth noting that whereas in the past Australian and other nations' drama educators have directed the spotlight on other countries, most notably England and Canada, for direction and insight, such dependence is fading (see Arnold and Taylor, 1995, for a further analysis of these trends).

Early progenitors and their legacy

While the beginnings of Western drama are tied into the wild dithyrambic festivals of ancient Greece, where gods of fertility were raised and celebrated, we note more didactic uses of the artform during the medieval period. In that time, theatreforms were deliberately solicited to teach or instruct. Acting out the passion of Christ and his followers, for example, was an instance of how the skills of the artist were pitched at influencing human behaviour in functional rather than aesthetic terms. The drama became the instrument though which cultural and religious understandings would be transmitted.

Within early twentieth-century school contexts we can count numerous examples of how this utilitarian function of drama became popular. Pioneers of drama in the language learning classroom, for example Caldwell Cook in England (1917), who worked at the Perse School in Cambridge, used drama strategies to engage students in their curriculum learning. In Cook's mind, drama was a powerful learning medium, a conduit through which information could be taught. However, Cook was not all that adept at communicating to his colleagues the learning outcomes. 'Visitors', writes one commentator, 'were surprised at the noise and the apparent disorder in the classroom and to find boys sitting on the desks and dangling their legs' (Allen, 1979, p. 11). Cook, like many drama educators who followed, found resistance to his methods. When a new headmaster arrived in 1928, Cook was told to 'stop all this nonsense'. Cook's methods, we are told, 'had no effect whatsoever on other admirable teachers of English on the staff' (ibid., p. 12).

In many respects, contemporary stereotypes of drama classrooms, seeming disorder, excitable behaviour and boisterous demonstrations, are confirmed by this early example of drama in schools. However, despite the stereotype, the common belief in countries like Australia and England during the 1960s and 1970s that drama tapped into the individual psyche and that human play and creative activity would release the unique self, fitted a child-centred approach to education and led to drama's heightened identity within school programmes, especially within language literacy contexts.

This period saw the beginning of many Australians and other nationals travelling to England to study with the distinguished drama educators Peter Slade, Brian Way, Dorothy Heathcote and Gavin Bolton.[1] Likewise, many English educators moved to Australia and North America and began to occupy leadership positions. The consequent growth in drama was staggering. At this same time, there was a chasm, as I argued in Chapter 1, developing within the field between those who espoused drama's power in pedagogical terms versus those who believed in its disciplinary potential: simply put, improvisational versus performance activity. The rancour between these camps reached such poisonous heights that programmes dedicated to drama and theatre education were cut (O'Brien and Dopierala, 1994, p. 24).

There have been many writers who separated drama as a learning medium from drama as an artform (Burgess and Gaudry, 1985; Burton, 1991; Deverall, 1981). The contributors to a recent anthology seem to share a belief that those who commit to drama as a powerful educative medium in the curriculum are denying access to a dramatic heritage. One contributor claims that Peter Slade, one of the first practitioners to emphasise the importance of dramatic play in young people's lives, did great harm to drama's status in the 1950s because he didn't promote the concept of a formal audience (see Gangi, 1998).

Simons (1992) has argued that this separation has not been a very helpful one for it has prevented those interested in pursuing improvisational activity in the classroom, sometimes likened to process drama practitioners, exploring what they have in common with theatre discipline. It is simply not correct to argue that those interested in pursuing the kind of drama praxis described in Chapter 1 are not interested in the dramatic artform. Indeed, it is the artform which powers the process.

Furthermore, the forced separation of product from process denied the eclectic work prevalent in most schools. 'Knowing what genres or dramatic forms are being explored in the theatre', argued Simons, 'can add to the range of forms being used' in improvisation (1992, p. 34), and vice versa. Although there is little indication that those practitioners married to the theatre are remotely interested in the drama praxis which occurs in schools. It is fair to say that in the past there had been a tendency for drama educators to present what they did in functional rather than aesthetic ways, and to remain aloof to the disciplinary roots of their subject's identity. There were clear historical trends and movements that made such divisions inevitable, the American creative drama movement being just one of these.

Creative drama

The genesis of creative drama in the United States is attributed to the work of Winifred Ward (1930, 1957) at Northwestern University in the early part of this century. Ward, influenced by Dewey (1921) and Mearns (1958), argued that creative drama developed the 'whole person' in that it benefited children's physical, intellectual, social, and emotional welfare:

 Its objectives are to give each child an avenue for self expression, guide his creative imagination, provide for a controlled emotional outlet, help him in the building of fine attitudes and appreciations and to give him opportunities to grow in social cooperation.

(Ward, 1957, p. 4)

Ward adopted a linear approach to lesson planning and proposed a sequential series of activities which children would typically encounter: 'the sequence proceeds from sensory/concentration activities to movement/pantomime, dialogue, characterisation, and improvisation/story playing' (Wright, 1985, p. 205).

Although it is difficult to generalise, creative drama sessions with children, as Ward construed them, often involved the dramatisation of stories. The group would plan in advance how they would enact each section of a story. Following the enactment, the group would evaluate their efforts: 'the building of the play demands keen thought and imagination, for it must be orderly, reasonable, convincing, permitting of no slipshod thinking and imagining' (Ward, 1930, p. 30). We have seen that these goals in lesson planning differ markedly from that of the drama praxis which Dorothy Heathcote pioneered. Ward was essentially interested in the power of creative drama in developing those personal and professional skills which she understood the society of her time deemed as important: skills related to communication, concentration, co-operation, tolerance, sensitivity, and trust. Although stressing an interest more in the process of creating a play with children rather than their performance of it, Ward, nevertheless, placed an emphasis on the external skills which children displayed through that process:

characterisation, development of plot, enriching of dialogue and action, ensemble work, and tempo are to be emphasised in class criticism, with voice and diction understood to be vitally important.

(Ward, 1930, p. 46)

Similar claims for creative drama are echoed in those who followed Ward (Heinig and Stillwell, 1981; McCaslin, 1981; Siks, 1983). Sixty years on, the influence of Ward's basic tenets of lesson planning are still advocated:

[the plan] will include stated objectives, warm-up activity, resource materials to be used, alternate resource materials which meet the same objectives, procedures, and warm down activity.

(Kase-Polisini, 1989, p. 134)

The leader's objectives, we further learn, 'relate to the development of each individual' and are 'based on predicted outcomes determined by the leader' (ibid., p. 105). A national review of this work emphasised the 'clarity and comprehensibility' in which 'those fundamental principles necessary to the creative drama process' were documented (Klein, 1990, p. 23).

Child drama and personal development

A contemporary of Ward's, Peter Slade (1954), introduced the concept 'child drama' in England. Rather than emphasising skills or a particular sequencing of activities, Slade stressed the child's natural impulses to create. Child drama, for Slade, was 'an art in itself'. The spontaneous impulses of the child to play had to be nurtured by the teacher, the latter being cast in the role of a 'loving ally'. In contrast to Ward's model, leaders would not, in theory, direct or criticise the students' drama, but rather they would cultivate in their classrooms moments of absorption and sincerity:

Absorption is being completely wrapped up in what is being done, or what one is doing, to the exclusion of all other thoughts . . . Sincerity is a complete form of honesty in portraying a part, bringing with it an intense feeling of reality and experience. (Slade, 1954, p. 2)

In this respect, Slade was highly critical of school plays which he argued stifled the child's innate creative urges. 'He deplored public performances,' Bolton argues, 'the proscenium arch, the use of scripts, the training of children to act, and, above all, teacher intervention in children's playing' (1985b, p. 153). The growing rift between drama and theatre has been partly attributed to the work of Slade.

In drawing a wedge between the school play and child play, Slade pre-empted the work of Brian Way (1967). Way, influenced by the progressive education movement of the 1960s, promoted drama on the basis that it developed what he called the 'individuality of the individual'. In emphasising personal and social 'life skills', he was sharing a common view with Ward. Consequently, it is perhaps not surprising that his text, *Development through Drama*, has been enormously influential in the US. His emphasis on the 'development of people' over the 'development of drama' led, however, to some bold claims:

> *whereas 'good' or 'exciting' or 'brilliant' drama does not necessarily prove that the people doing it are good or exciting or brilliant, nevertheless 'fully developed' people will seldom make poor or uninteresting drama, even though it may not be brilliant.* (Way, 1967, p. 2)

'Fully developed' people, it seemed, were characterised by their sensitivity, trust, understanding, and co-operation, rather than by their adeptness at producing 'brilliant' drama. Critics might ask, how does one determine shades of 'good', 'exciting', or 'brilliant'? Whether or not drama can or should have a particular claim to developing these qualities has been questioned (Bolton, 1985a). Yet it was evident that Way's typical drama teacher, tambour usually in hand, leading the group through a sequence of 'direct, nonsymbolic, sensory experiences', now had a secure base of exercises which the class could enact (Bolton, 1985b, p. 154).

Although there have been other offshoots of drama praxis, the influences of Ward, Slade and Way are important signposts when considering the approach to drama promoted in this text. Each of these writers portrayed a view of drama and proposed pedagogical functions which run counter to those suggested by Dorothy Heathcote.

Dorothy Heathcote and drama praxis

By the early 1950s, as Ward's approach to creative drama was dominating US praxis, Heathcote was just commencing her career as a lecturer in drama at Newcastle University in England. Unlike Ward, Heathcote maintained that the passion of drama was not bound by narrative: 'Drama is not stories retold in action. Drama is human beings confronted by situations which change them because of what they must face in dealing with those challenges' (Heathcote, 1967, p. 48). Heathcote was particularly interested in how the artform of drama could be exploited by the teacher and students to explore important issues, events, or relationships. This notion of drama as exploration, or as a 'learning medium' (Wagner, 1999b), was a prominent aim of her work and distinguishes it from that of her predecessors. Ward's understanding of passion emphasised the re-enactment of storylines, and the conflicts that emerged from them. Heathcote's understanding of passion emphasised the dilemmas participants encountered when trapped within the imaginary world.

Heathcote's idea of passion in drama would focus on moments in time which the group would devise, rather than Ward's dramatised plot scenarios contained in stories already written:

> *Dramatic improvisation is concerned with what we discover for our-selves and the group when we place ourselves in a human situation containing some element of desperation. Very simply it means putting yourself into other people's shoes and, by using personal experience to help you to understand their point of view, you may discover more than you knew when you started.* (Heathcote, 1967, p. 44)

Developing 'understanding', however, would not happen by chance, Heathcote argued. If the passion in drama was about discovery, then activities or strategies would need to be deliberately and consciously folded, or layered, into the work for this to happen. The fact that the teacher and students should ideally be operating at a meta-cognitive level implied in her mind a 'structure'. Although not denying the value of spontaneity in dramatic activity, her interest in exploring the consequences of actions when participants are put in 'other people's shoes' indicated a different pedagogical emphasis from that of her predecessors. 'Teachers who for years had planned in terms of appropriate actions', Bolton argued, were now challenged by Heathcote to think of the 'appropriate meanings' of those actions (Bolton, 1984, p. 53). The implications of actions became, then, in Heathcote's mind, just as important as the dramatic action itself. Although Heathcote has not authored a book herself, her work has been described in detail by an American, B. J. Wagner (1999b), and her selected writings and papers have been assembled in an anthology (Johnson and O'Neill, 1984). With her colleague Gavin Bolton, her pioneering technique, mantle of the expert, has been de-constructed and examined (Heathcote and Bolton, 1995). Her considerable influence on drama praxis is indicated by the volume of international interest. Prominent Canadian (Booth, 1987; Morgan and Saxton, 1987; Swartz, 1995), Australian (Burgess and Gaudry, 1985; O'Toole, 1992) and British (Byron, 1986; Fines and Verriour, 1974; Neelands, 1990) educators have gleaned pedagogical principles from her work.

One of the more radical ways in which Heathcote transformed approaches to drama praxis was the manner in which she would play along with the students in a drama, usually by adopting a role herself. While creative drama as 'an improvisational, non-exhibitional, process-centred form of drama' (Davis and Behm, 1978, p. 10) supports many of Heathcote's aims, it was in this domain of teacher role-play which presupposed a different function of drama.

Ward and Way suggested that the teacher guide or lead from outside the drama experience. Slade saw the teacher more as a facilitator who provided the forum for children to play; yet still the teacher would facilitate from a non-participatory perspective. To halt or in any way interfere with children's play, Slade argued, would be tainting or spoiling their creativity. Heathcote, however, claimed that as drama was about human dilemmas, then the work must be structured in ways that the implications of people's actions can be explored fully. She challenged the notion of uninterrupted, free, and spontaneous play, and she advocated planning for reflection in drama. Teachers, she urged, should structure strategies through which experiences in drama can be examined: one key structural strategy was the teacher in role.

This technique fundamentally distinguishes her approach from the creative drama teacher. McCaslin (1990) argued that 'the majority of American creative drama teachers . . . rarely . . . take an active part' in the imaginary world (p. 292). We have already seen that creative drama teachers emphasised skill development rather than the reflection on experiences. Heathcote, on the other hand, was concerned with structuring so that participants discover more about themselves and their 'habitual orientation to the world' (O'Neill,

1990, p. 293). Structuring from inside the drama was one aspect of this approach.

There has been much resistance among creative drama practitioners to the idea of teachers working within the dramatic context. Rosenberg (1987) likens such role-play to teachers' inclinations to reveal their acting prowess or their subconscious desires to 'hide for a time behind another identity' (p. 37). Other commentators have construed in-role teaching as acting or character portrayal (Kase-Polisini, 1989; McCaslin, 1990). These commentators tend to negate the pedagogical function which Heathcote initially intended. O'Neill neatly summarises this purpose:

> *When a teacher works in role it is an act of conscious self-presentation, but one which invites the watchers – the students – to respond actively, to join in, to oppose or transform what is happening. The teacher-in-role unites the students, trades on their feelings of ambivalence and vulnerability and focuses their attention.* (O'Neill, 1989, p. 535)

Although teachers can structure the work from within rather than direct from the outside, they should always, it is claimed, be alert to their functional role. They are 'emphatically not acting' but conscious of how they might enable participants to explore the issue, event, or relationship under investigation (O'Neill, 1991, p. 4).

Heathcote was one of the first drama practitioners to suggest this pedagogical function of structural operator. Ideally, however, in her mind all classroom participants are involved with designing, developing, or structuring the experience. If not, O'Neill argues, 'this would result in a kind of teacher-controlled drama dictation lesson' (O'Neill, 1991, p. 4). Drama praxis should involve a partnership forged between teachers and students to construct an imaginary world for reflection. This purpose then poses a different set of demands to lesson planning or structuring as compared with those creative drama specialists face.

According to one commentator, a creative drama teacher's lesson plans typically adopt the following framework: 'groups begin with simple rhythm and movement, using theatre games and exercises. They move to simple pantomime working on sensory training' (Kase-Polisini, 1989, p. 142). The teacher's agenda is paramount in this plan. However, when teachers are negotiating and co-creating the content with their students, and thereby jointly acting as structural operators, it is impossible to predetermine all the steps. A feature of Heathcote's drama praxis is the manner in which it gradually evolves:

 if the event is to remain genuinely improvisatory, implying spontane-ity, uncertainty, ingenuity, exploration and discovery, the sequences of episodes or scenes will not be predetermined, but discovered.

(O'Neill, 1991, p. 4)

Bolton (1985a) has argued that one of the difficulties which teachers face when structuring drama has 'to do with creating an experience that is credible enough or deeply moving enough' for participants to engage in it (p. 12). Teachers, therefore, in moving towards this credible experience, will need to adjust their strategies based on the 'here and now' encounters which their group faces during the drama. Because Heathcote's understanding of passion works on the premise that the group is continually creating the imaginary experience, it is impossible for the teacher or students to predict what this shared experience may entail. Classroom dynamics can obviously have an impact on the structure's development. Participants' differing interests, attitudes, and personalities can influence how the structure evolves (Bolton, 1980, p. 167).

Structural decisions are often made during the passion. Teachers, therefore, require an ability to improvise the structure as it unfolds. The intended focus may shift. The group might move towards a different domain from what was originally intended.

Critics of Heathcote's praxis

 While some drama educationalists undoubtedly believe that the evan-gelism of charismatic workshop performers like Dorothy Heathcote marked a radical break with the past, I would argue that the methodo-logy popularised by Heathcote and her amanuenses has inherited all the worst characteristics of school drama's progressivist legacy.

(Hornbrook, 1991, p. 19)

In recent years, there has been concern that Heathcote's emphasis on method has done much harm in England to the disciplinary status of drama. The debate in England has been particularly fierce, with theatre and drama people lining up in virtual camps and firing salvos. The main leader of the theatre movement was the one time 'actor' and 'director', David Hornbrook.

Hornbrook argued that the emphasis on drama as a learning or pedagogical medium has 'denied students access to the culture and skills of the theatre'. In what sounds reminiscent of E. D. Hirsh (1987), he mourns the fact that England, which has 'one of the richest theatrical traditions in the world', has managed to produce 'a generation of students who are, in effect, dramatically illiterate' (1991, p. 21). Literacy, in this sense, seems to imply that canon of theatrical masterpieces which a dominant cultural group judges as important, a definition which would be subject to a range of interpretations at any given time. In a recent text, he argues that the purpose of drama education is 'cultural induction' (1998, p. 15). The term 'cultural induction' is left uncritiqued. He blames Heathcote and her 'proselytes' for the 'impoverishment' of drama education, and particularly he cites Bolton's and O'Neill's uncritical analysis of her work as evidence of this lack.

Hornbrook's idea of an effective drama class is one which 'must restore the dramatic product to a central position'. When Heathcote aims to collaborate with her students, Hornbrook argues that teachers 'must ensure that [they] are taught what they need to make progress' (1991, p. 22). Hornbrook demands 'attainment targets' in drama, whereas Heathcote appeals for 'authentic experiences'. Hornbrook finds such descriptions 'mystifying' ([1989] 1998, p. 18). In his role as an arts inspector, he argued that 'a knowledge-based curriculum' which addresses the 'inspectors' concerns over purpose and progression' is required (1998, p. 15). When Heathcote speaks of negotiating the curriculum, Hornbrook proposes 'a field of knowledge, understanding and skills which constitutes drama as a discipline' (1991, p. 21). Both seem to have a different perception of praxis, of how a curriculum should be constructed.

Not only have Heathcote's methodological emphases been criticised, but so too has her own perceived 'dominating and manipulative' personality (Errington, 1992). Bolton (1985b) suggests that for many drama educators who believed, like Hornbrook, that there is a body of theatrical knowledge to be taught, it was difficult for them to comprehend the different paradigm from which Heathcote worked.

The notion, for example, of the teacher assuming a role and co-creating with the students led to one commentator asking, 'Is this drama?' (Faulkes-Jendyk, 1975). For teachers used to putting students in small groups so that they could make and perform plays, or for those drama specialists who emphasised the annual school musical, it was perhaps unsurprising that Heathcote's focus on whole group exploration, which would not be performed in the school auditorium for the community, might be controversial.

Although Hornbrook likens all those who have found Heathcote's techniques useful to showing 'a puritanical disdain for all the things that actually make theatre *theatre* – actors, theatres and plays' (1991, p. 21), in his recent publications he has made no attempt to address any of the criticisms of his own theories (1998 and [1989] 1998), criticisms which focus on his emphasis on Western notions of functional literacy, cultural heritage, and his need for neo-positivistic outcomes. It's like he has lived in a time warp since 1989, failing to advance the terrain of his own praxis.

A shared mission

Despite the difference in approaches and the infighting that has occurred in the field, each of the pioneering authors shares a belief in the power of drama to transform human behaviour. While drama is different from most school learning given its use of role-relationships, time and space dimensions, focus and tension, its capacity to realise and reveal the unconscious memory, and probe that which is conscious, has been claimed as its strengths by its proponents.

A richness in drama praxis arises from the revelations, the tensions and the unconscious interpretations revealed through the interpersonal dynamics. Often, it is the unconscious material arising from drama praxis which signifies its educative power. Research has begun to address the manifestation of the unconscious slips of the tongue, the unexpected emphases, the spontaneous movements and gestures, and the significant proxemics between characters and the meaningful silences. What was formerly concealed is now revealed, what was unspoken is now spoken, and what was unembodied in the unconscious is now embodied (see Taylor, 1996).

Note

1 See Resources section.

References

ALLEN, J. (1979) *Drama in Schools: Its Theory and Practice*, London: Heinemann.

ARNOLD, R. and TAYLOR, P. (1995) 'Drama in education: assuming the centre stage', *Forum of Education*, **50**, 2, pp. 19–27.

BOLTON, G. (1980) 'Theatre form in drama teaching', in D. DAVIS and C. LAWRENCE (eds) (1986) *Gavin Bolton: Selected Writings on Drama in Education*, London: Longman, pp. 164–180.

BOLTON, G. (1984) *Drama as Education*, Harlow: Longman.

BOLTON, G. (1985a) Gavin Bolton interviewed by David Davis, *2D*, **4**, 2, pp. 4–14.

BOLTON, G. (1985b) 'Changes in thinking about drama in education', *Theory into Practice*, **XXIV**, 3, pp. 151–157.

BOOTH, D. (1987) *Drama Words*, Toronto: Language Study Centre.

BRITTON, J. (1971) *Language and Learning*, Harmondsworth: Penguin.

BRUNER, J. (1979) *On Knowing: Essays for the Left Hand*, Cambridge, Mass.: Harvard University Press.

BURGESS, R. and GAUDRY, R. (1985) *Time for Drama*, Philadelphia: Open University.

BURTON, B. (1991) *The Act of Learning*, Melbourne: Longman.

BYRON, K. (1986) *Drama in the English Classroom*, New York: Methuen.

COOK, C. (1917) *The Play Way*, Portsmouth, N.H.: Heinemann.

DAVIS, J. and BEHM, T. (1978) 'Terminology of drama/theatre with and for children', *Children's Theatre Review*, **27**, 1, pp. 10–11.

DEVERALL, J. (1981) 'Playing the game: play games and drama', *The NADIE Journal*, **6**, 2, pp. 36–40.

DEWEY, J. (1921) *The School and Society*, Chicago: University of Chicago Press.

DIXON, J. (1967) *Growth through English*, London: Oxford University Press.

ERRINGTON, E. (1992) *Towards a Socially Critical Drama Education*, Geelong: Deakin University.

FAULKES-JENDYK, M. (1975) 'Creative dramatic leaders face objective examination', in *Canadian Child and Youth Drama Association Bulletin*, Toronto, pp. 6–7.

FINES, J. and VERRIOUR, R. (1974) *The Drama of History*, London: New University Education.

GANGI, J. (1998) 'Making sense of drama in an electronic age', in D. HORNBROOK (ed.) *On the Subject of Drama*, London: Routledge.

HEATHCOTE, D. (1967) 'Improvisation', in L. JOHNSON and C. O'NEILL (1984) *Dorothy Heathcote: Collected Writings on Education and Drama*, London, Hutchinson, pp. 44–48.

HEATHCOTE, D. (1980) *Drama as Context*, Aberdeen: National Association for Teaching of English.

HEATHCOTE, D. and BOLTON, G. (1995) *Drama for Learning: Dorothy Heathcote's Mantle of the Expert Approach to Education*, Portsmouth, N.H.: Heinemann.

HEINIG, R. B. and STILLWELL, L. (1981) *Creative Drama for the Classroom Teacher*, Engleword Cliffs, N.J.: Prentice-Hall.

HIRSCH, E. D. (1987) *Cultural Literacy*, Boston, Mass.: Houghton Mifflin.

HORNBROOK, D. ([1989] 1998) *Education and Dramatic Art* (2nd edn), London: Routledge.

HORNBROOK, D. (1991) *Education in Drama*, London: Falmer.

HORNBROOK, D. (ed.) (1998) *On the Subject of Drama*, London: Routledge.

HUGHES, J. (1988) 'Educational drama in a climate of educational change', *The NADIE Journal*, **13**, 1, pp. 2–4.

JOHNSON, L. and O'NEILL, C. (eds) (1984) *Dorothy Heathcote: Collected Writings on Drama in Education*, London: Hutchinson.

KASE-POLISINI, J. (1989) *The Creative Drama Book: Three Approaches*, New Orleans, La.: Anchorage.

KLEIN, J. (1990) 'Books in review', *Youth Theatre Journal*, **4**, 3, pp. 22–23.

McCASLIN, N. (ed.) (1981) *Children and Drama* (2nd edn), New York: Longman.

McCASLIN, N. (1990) *Creative Drama in the Classroom* (5th edn), New York: Longman.

MANLEY, A. and O'NEILL, C. (1995) *Dreamseekers: Creative Approaches to the African American Heritage*, Portsmouth, N.H.: Heinemann.

MEARNS, H. (1958) *Creative Power* (2nd rev. edn), New York: Dover.

MOFFETT, J. (1968) *Teaching the Universe of Discourse*, Boston, Mass.: Houghton Mifflin.

MORGAN, N. and SAXTON, J. (1987) *Teaching Drama*, London: Hutchinson.

NEELANDS, J. (1990) *Structuring Drama Work*, Cambridge: Cambridge University Press.

O'BRIEN, A. and DOPIERALA, W. (1994) *The Pleasure of the Company: Drama and Teacher Education at Melbourne 1961–1994*, Melbourne: The University of Melbourne.

O'NEILL, C. (1989) 'Dialogue and drama: the transformation of events, ideas and teachers', *Language Arts*, **66**, 5, pp. 528–540.

O'NEILL, C. (1990) 'Drama as a significant experience', in N. MCCASLIN, *Creative Drama in the Classroom* (5th edn), New York: Longman, pp. 293–295.

O'NEILL, C. (1991) 'Dramatic worlds: structuring for significant experience', *The Drama/Theatre Teacher*, **4**, 1, pp. 3–5.

O'TOOLE, J. (1992) *The Process of Drama*, London: Routledge.

ROSENBERG, H. (1987) *Creative Drama and Imagination: Transforming Ideas into Action*, New York: Holt, Rinehart & Winston.

SIKS, G. (1983) *Drama with Children* (2nd edn), New York: Harper & Row.

SIMONS, J. (1992) 'Bridging the gap: adolescent plays', *The NADIE Journal*, **16**, 3, pp. 31–34.

SLADE, P. (1954) *Child Drama*, London: University of London Press.

SWARTZ, L. (1995) *Dramathemes*, Portsmouth, N.H.: Heinemann.

TAYLOR, P. (ed.) (1996) *Researching Drama and Arts Education: Paradigms and Possibilities*, London: Falmer.

VYGOTSKY, L. (1978) *Mind in Society: The Development of Higher Psychological Processes*, Cambridge, Mass.: Harvard University Press.

WAGNER, B. J. (1998) *Educational Drama and Language Arts: What Research Shows*, Portsmouth, N.H.: Heinemann.

WAGNER, B. J. (ed.) (1999a) *Building Moral Communities through Educational Drama*, Stamford, Conn.: Ablex.

WAGNER, B. J. (1999b) *Dorothy Heathcote: Drama as a Learning Medium* (rev. edn), Portland, Me.: Calender Islands Publishers.

WARD, W. (1930) *Creative Dramatics*, New York: Appleton.

WARD, W. (1957) *Playmaking for Children*, New York: Appleton.

WAY, B. (1967) *Development Through Drama*, London: Longman.

WINSTON, J. (1998) *Drama, Narrative and Moral Education: Exploring Traditional Tales in the Primary Years*, London: Falmer.

WRIGHT, L. (1985) 'Preparing teachers to put drama in the classroom', *Theory into Practice*, **XXIV**, 3, pp. 205–209.

Chapter 6	Building and assessing effective partnerships: action, reflection, transformation

In the opening chapter I argued how the elements of drama involved an artistic manipulation of three elements: people, passion and a platform. In effect, these three elements are partnered together as teachers generate powerful aesthetic experiences. However, we could also say that a wider partnership is necessary if drama praxis is to be managed well, a partnership not only between the three elements but between teachers, their students, the school community, and the various administrative agencies that can support the arts in education.

In this concluding chapter I will examine how drama praxis can create satisfying partnerships. I will return to the key principles of drama praxis as outlined in Chapter 1, and demonstrate how successful partnerships in drama praxis enable the stakeholders:

■ **to activate** themselves as artist-educators,
■ **to reflect** upon their own contribution to the partnership, and
■ **to transform** their own understanding of themselves and the world in which they live.

Partnerships in the arts provide experiences which change and transform us, experiences which provoke good and sometimes unsettling questions, experiences which both please and educate. As one of the key conditions for a successful partnership lay in the power of the artwork created, my discussion shall begin with how the artwork can engage participants so that a successful partnership can emerge.

A satisfying artwork

Some years back I was involved in co-organising an international symposium on aesthetic education which examined the critical function the artwork presents, whether that be through a performance or in a process drama, in facilitating a successful educational partnership.[1] What does an artwork need to contain if it is to satisfy those who experience it?

The three works which were explored at the symposium challenged the audience to interrogate the qualities of artistic praxis. The works were STREB, an American postmodern dance; THE DIVINE KISS, a multi-arts contemporary Australian opera, featuring intellectually and physically challenged actors; and KILL EVERYTHING YOU LOVE, a play about self-destruction of youths written by a young Australian playwright.

There was much heated conversation among symposium delegates about whether these works were artistic. I remember prominent figures in the international arts community claiming that STREB, for instance, was merely acrobatics with a twist. Others saw different possibilities as the dancers threw themselves into walls, and were catapulted into the air by rotating beams, on a human journey, as it were, to break the physical boundaries which entrap us.

It was Maxine Greene who reminded us that in aesthetic education we are seeking new perspectives, we are breaking with the familiar, the mundane. For Greene, STREB's performance made her rethink space and gravity, and helped her contemplate how dancers reach beyond where they normally are, how their/our bodies define the spaces we inhabit and the spaces we strive to reach. Greene explained that what she hopes the arts might achieve in education is helping teachers and their students confront themselves:

> *I have hopes always that if teachers are awakened, if teachers become more imaginative, if teachers face the darkness and the ambiguities of their own lives, something about what they have become may become contagious when they are in the classroom, when they are working with artists or when they are working with performances.*[2]

We had similar conversations about the artfulness of THE DIVINE KISS, a visually striking piece which focused on the seven saving virtues.

As actors swept toy dolls from the performance space, and while the audience was deluged by blinding sparks as they discovered an actor in a firestorm, I tried to unfathom the significance of these images. I thought it clever of the director to cast a blind actor singing of hope on a starlit night while standing beside a baby's cot and telescope, but I wondered too about the artistic merits.

And as my doubts grew I was again reminded of Greene who has pleaded that we remain open to the work, that we let the images massage our senses:

 We have to realise that if we are trying to release children to become what they are not yet, to be free, to explore, to discover, by releasing children to move into the unknown, we can't tell them where to go – we just have to rejoice that they are alive . . . [if] a kind of wide-awakeness can develop through the partnership, the better chance that we have that children will wake up and rebel against dullness and boredom and repetitiveness and the mechanical life. I like to spend my life fighting the anaesthetic. You know, the numbness, the dullness, the refusal to respond to the couch potato syndrome, so that children can see more, and feel more, and hear more, and reach further, and maybe become something more than what they call human resources for other people to mould.[3]

It is inevitable that my response to THE DIVINE KISS is centred within my understanding of theatreform, and by how I read the seven saving virtues. Yet it is also shaped by how I read disability, by what I believe constitutes human perfection. If, as Bernard Beckerman (1970), the great drama theorist says, drama is always in a state of becoming, and that we who are encountering works of art are caught in situations which we must work our way out of, I feel I am still trapped by THE DIVINE KISS, struggling to penetrate its layered meanings.

I think it is interesting that *partnership* contains within it the word ART: p*art*nership. The most satisfying artworks are structured so that audiences interact, they engage with a work's aesthetic possibilities, become active participants who join with the art object, encountering it from their own perspective, and based on the kinds of experiences they have had. The artwork is powered by a dynamic encounter between the work (whether that be the object itself or the drama process) and those who experience it.

Partnerships cannot be forced in the arts and they certainly cannot be forced in drama classrooms. I cannot insist that my students have satisfying experiences, but I must structure the work in a way that satisfaction might emerge. And knowledge of satisfaction is based on experience, education and discipline. Experience has told us that leaders who take no account of their audiences, who fail to acknowledge their context, might fall into some very dangerous traps. I was heartened to hear Roddy Doyle, the Irish author, say on an English interview show that his primary concern as a high school teacher for twelve years was to keep the students interested, to entertain them if you like (see Merkin, 1999). Which made me think of the British educator Dorothy Heathcote, who, we are told, pioneered the teacher-in-role strategy initially because she needed to focus the students' attention, and she thought she could most effectively do that by shaping the form and content from within the drama. Thus, a new teaching technique emerges from experience (see Bolton, 1998, for a rich analysis of Heathcote's praxis).

Often the most effective teachers, not just drama teachers, are able to see themselves as working in partnership with their students. Cecily O'Neill (1995) uses the perceptive image of effective teachers being able to lead the way while walking backwards. Leaders, she argues, will need to act as guides who should know where the travellers have come from, and the nature of the journey so far, so that they can help shape the kind of journey which lies ahead. Rather than leading with their backs to the students, leaders face students while moving forward, conscious of where the group are at, and what they are capable of achieving. *Walking backwards to the future* is a delightful metaphor in describing good partnerships in the drama classroom. Teachers, though, have not always construed of their praxis in this manner.

The 1970s drama teacher

I well recall my own early years as a seventh-grade drama student in an Australian high school. The classroom I experienced in the early 1970s was characterised by a different conception of the leader from that which O'Neill suggests above. Picture, if you will, a classroom isolated from the main school building, a portable room separated from the other teaching spaces. As the children enter this blackened-out space, they notice a figure standing in a kaftan by the hi-fi system, assorting and selecting records. This teacher looks like he might have just entered from a hippie commune, adorned as he is with beads while the kaleidoscopic patterns on his outfit seem to beckon the students in.

'Come in and get ready, my treasures', the teacher would say, as me and my classmates enthusiastically would prepare ourselves, changing into our free flowing gear, removing our shoes, going through the required rituals as we prepared for drama.

'Now, find your own space and lie down', he would add, fascinated by the record sleeves he was holding, meticulously taking each one out of the box and contemplating its dramatic possibilities. And so we would separate around the room eager to begin the familiar routine of our drama class. 'Okay, now focus on your breathing, centre those breaths. Hands on your diaphragm.' He would walk around the room now. 'Eyes shut now, settle down. Concentrate.' Concentrate was the common instruction of the 1970s.

We had this view that the drama teacher was the expert, a mystical figure what's more, whose soft and gently spoken instructions we would willingly obey. 'Now, imagine you are lying on a beach. My, the sun feels good doesn't it, as it massages your body.' As the students enjoyed the sensations, the teacher provided an affirming comment, 'You feel like you are sinking through the sand, you are so relaxed.'

Little did we know that the restful and soothing nature of our contemplations were soon to be horribly transformed. 'The sun is now wrenching hot, and you feel your body starting to sweat all over', the teacher would sternly say. 'You are grossly uncomfortable as you try and fight your way out of this suffocation but, oh no,' he quickly added, 'someone has shackled your ankles and wrists, you can't move. You scream for help, but you have no voice.'

And as our anxiety grew and our bodies gyrated with all the intensity of people who have been trapped against their will, the leader finally said: 'And the shackles are removed. Relax. Feel yourself sinking again. Centre your breathing, in, then out.' After a minute or so we would be asked to sit up in our own time. 'In your own time', was a frequent teacher directive as well.

'Come over to me', he would then wave, 'and listen attentively.' He had selected the record he was to play, *Peter and the Wolf*, a particular favourite, old but definitely still popular in the early 1970s: 'I want you to imagine that you are going on a trip through the magical forest. You must first get ready, pack your bags, get your supplies together.' And as we mimicked getting ready for an adventure, our teacher, noticeably happy with our efforts, would add, 'We are now ready for our journey.' We then enacted the teacher's narrative of going through the forest while the selected music served as a backdrop. He would remind us that in this particular setting we were likely to come across the most amazing creatures, 'Each more amazing with every turn along the forest's path.' As readers can imagine, we demonstrated the appropriate emotions at the required sections: fear, relief and joy being just three of them.

And then, the major theme of the session would be introduced, usually the theme would focus on a topical issue, such as advertising. A lot of our work in the 1970s was issue based. As the teacher shared with us magazine pages of how companies marketed their products, we became amused at the familiar ploys of advertisers to gain our attention: the sparkling smiling white teeth for a new brand of toothpaste, the conventional nuclear family munching on their healthy breakfast, the slim attractive couple in their new denim jeans.

Our task for the lesson would be to work in small groups and incorporate some of these devices to market a new product for a television commercial. Yes, highly entertaining for participants and audience. On a good day all of the group work would be shared and our lesson would close with another relaxation exercise, usually lying on the floor with our breathing being the focus. My teacher was always concerned that we demonstrated the appropriate signals of being relaxed, which meant that our palms had to be facing up. He knew we weren't relaxed if, when he came to lift our arms, they would not be limp. 'You're not relaxed', he would note, unhappily, to the offenders.

I remember describing this familiar experience of a drama class in the 1970s for a large group of teachers at an Australian state conference recently, and being rebuked by a group of three women for satirising their own classroom work. Clearly, such a classroom pattern is still in evidence today. And while I do not want to undermine this style of teaching, it is difficult to characterise this way of working as a partnership between the teachers and students. Teachers, it seems, did not necessarily see themselves as being partnered with their students in the 1970s.

In Bolton's 1979 book, *Towards a Theory of Drama in Education*, he deconstructs this kind of teaching and how it was motivated by having students mindlessly pursue the dictated steps of the teacher. One problem with this lesson is that there is no logic to it, the bits are not coherently linked. In some respects, this style of teaching reminds me of the well-oiled aerobics lesson, popular in the 1980s, and which, ironically, I was very much into at the time. We have the familiar warm up common to both. In the drama lesson it included stock physical exercises, which became predictable after some time. Movement and voice exercises were the staple. Head rolls, for example, were popular, popular even in the aerobic class, I might add.

The main activity in the aerobics lesson would be the intensive cardiovascular workout which included lots of jumping and running. In the drama lesson, we were usually put into groups and made up mini-plays based on stimulus material given by the teacher. And the closure in the drama class, called the cool-down in aerobics, would include numerous relaxation exercises, again dictated by the leader. Just as Bolton has argued how flawed this kind of structure can be, it is interesting that fitness groups distanced themselves by the end of the 1980s from the ankle-jarring, bone-crushing routines of the typical aerobic session, preferring more low-impact workouts which were seen as less physically damaging. Head rolls, for instance, we learnt caused considerable damage to people's necks if not executed correctly. I am still troubled today where I observe intense physical warm-ups of drama classes where harmful routines can be seen.

Just as there is little in the way of joint sharing between teachers and their students in this praxis, there is little partnering between the gym instructor and the client. Although signs of 1970s teaching are still evident, the field has moved considerably as it incorporates the voices and minds of all students into the evolution of the drama class. Common sense suggests that students are more likely to commit when they are actively involved in initiating and shaping content and form.

Partnerships which are built on notions of expertise limit the control participants have when collaborating with teachers. Traditionally in the drama class, students put themselves in the teacher's hands and in doing so gain a sense of security based on faith. Ironically, teachers, too, put themselves in other professionals' hands, often repeating activities that they have been taught by others, or which they have learnt elsewhere. The praxis described in this book recognises that while the teacher is a leader informed by good praxis, the created work demands the input and control of all those involved with it.

In innovative partnerships, students should join with their teachers, share their knowledge, and in doing so gain a sense of increased power. We must work against the dominant model in traditional classrooms, where students are satisfied that their interests are being looked after, and that they only need comply with the advice of their leaders and all will be well. It can be educationally damaging when we perpetuate a notion that the experts will look after us. Experts can be wrong, and can lead us astray.

In innovative partnerships, all parties should exercise control over the situation. There is camaraderie forged between teachers and their participants as they work together, acting as mutual collaborators. As Freire (1970) argues, when teachers can engage in authentic dialogue with their students, the students will become self-reliant and a more equitable sharing of power emerges:

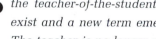 *the teacher-of-the-students and the students-of-the-teacher cease to exist and a new term emerges: teacher-student with student-teacher. The teacher is no longer merely the one who teaches, but one who is himself taught in dialogue with the students, who, in their turn, while being taught, also teach.* (Freire, 1970, p. 67)

Good drama praxis works towards a joint partnership where knowledge, talents and skills are shared.

Action, reflection, transformation: effective partnerships

I'd like to conclude by examining three different examples of partnerships which are, in my view, innovative. I do not think it is

possible that we can divorce partnerships from the context in which they occur. As readers may know, I have a strong commitment to qualitative research, and a principal concern of this method is to acknowledge the environment in which the work takes place.
Each of these examples are situated in what we might describe as economically impoverished/depressed areas, so the context for good partnerships is not dependent on there being socio-economic privileges.

I Partnerships activate participants to believe in their own worth

Not long ago, I was mentoring a teacher one day a week in Regata, an Australian suburb on the far outskirts of a major city. I was collaborating in partnership with this teacher, who I'll call Jenny, and her Grade 5/6 composite class (ten–twelve-year-olds). I had never visited Regata before this partnership, although I carried with me my own stereotypes of the area.

Urban development only began in Regata after the Second World War where the farming land was divided into urban lots which the returning soldiers could purchase at low prices. The government's plan was to locate workers' housing near the agricultural industry. While this strategy led to a fairly close-knit community in Regata with a high level of local pride, it was troubled by geographic isolation and limited access to employment, shopping and other essential services. As Jenny said to me when first we met, 'You never tell anyone you are from Regata because they go, "Oh, no!" But if you tell them you are next door, well that's not so bad.'

Jenny would tell me how many of the families of the Regata schoolchildren are single parented, with over 50 per cent dependent on social security. Education did not seem to be valued in the community which was, in part, demonstrated by Jenny's observation that the local shopping centre in Regata did not have a bookshop, and for many of these children that shopping centre is where their lives are centred outside of school.

The school seemed in definite need of a facelift, with buildings in disarray and temporary masonite structures in abundance. Some buildings had not been painted in twenty-five years. I couldn't help but contrast this site to other schools I had been to where facilities were first rate and resources of the highest calibre.

I was there on Jenny's invitation. While the school did receive one or two visits from an arts council each year there was little dedication given to the arts in Regata School. Jenny wanted to include more drama in the curriculum, but she lacked confidence. I was surprised at her admission given that she had completed a semester of drama education in her undergraduate teacher-training degree. As she was to say, 'I want to incorporate it [drama], but I don't know how to do it in a meaningful way.' I just happened to be in my office when Jenny phoned, asking if someone from my university could assist her design drama in the curriculum.

One of the traps for teachers like Jenny is to place the onus of expertise on to the visitor. In other words, it was possible that Jenny was hoping that I would lead the drama, and she would just observe it. Jenny did explain that her experience of visiting arts agencies, such as theatre in education teams, was that they would do all the work. Obviously, Jenny was not going to be activated in this form of partnership, she merely becomes the recipient of other people's curriculum.

A principle of effective partnerships is to empower the classroom teacher to believe in their own worth, to activate their own capacity to influence and direct curriculum. Jenny was not going to be liberated in her drama teaching if I came in as the expert who conducted her drama lessons, then retired to the university while she retired to her normal curriculum. Jenny's teaching would not be liberated if the visitor was put into the authoritative role. She had to have her authority elevated in the partnership. The trick was to press steps into the work where Jenny could jointly construct, implement and evaluate the sessions.

It was agreed from the beginning that Jenny would have responsibility for leading the work in the latter half of the residence. Further, while I would assume responsibility for initiating the drama in its early phases, I wanted to work within her own curriculum and share with her my planning. So if she was studying bushrangers or ancient legends then I would construct sessions with her around these topics and make her familiar with the learning outcomes being sought. As well, I would encourage her to initiate tasks, to step into role, and facilitate discussions with her students.

And what a joy it was to watch her in action as she took the lead. When she decided, towards the end of my residence at Regata, that she was going to design her drama praxis on the topic 'The Vikings', I sat mesmerised as she began in role with her students: 'I do believe a team of archaeologists are about to make a great find, because a village in Yorkshire, where you are, is rumoured to have once had Vikings settle there.' She knew that one of the most effective aspects of drama praxis was that it puts students on the inside of their learning, and that by framing a drama on the Vikings with the students as archaeologists who are attempting to unravel the past, motivates the students to act as detectives who must solve a mystery.

And with that beginning, she and her students, now in role as archaeologists, created an archaeological dig in Yorkshire. She continued:

'We must be very careful and unearth the soil gently. We have to find pieces of past life. Find your brushes and small tools. Find a place to dig. What might you discover?' Her classroom was transported into a beavering of activity where the archaeologists discovered swords, daggers, bones from bodies.

'No jewels on this dagger', said one lad.

'So it didn't belong to anyone rich', added Jenny.

As the archaeologists shared their discoveries, Jenny, now out of role, described her actual visit to the Yorkshire Archaeological Museum, and she told the class about the petrified faeces in the museum, and how in Viking times moss and leaves were used as toilet paper. The archaeologists were disgusted by this observation, but their fascination with the period was launched.

As I left that school on my last visit, Jenny said she would carry on with the work. 'Drama will now be part of their programme', were her final words to me. The partnership had helped her recognise her own strengths and build up her confidence.

2 Partnerships reflect on 'What is happening now?'

I've been collaborating with pre-kindergarten teachers in the Rustic section of Brooklyn, New York.[4] I'd like to share observations they have made about how to work in partnership with visiting teaching artists; observations which focus especially on their own elevation as artist educators through the partnership.

Rustic, Brooklyn is a fascinating area. I'll never forget my first experience of the neighbourhood while I was walking to the school where my host, the Creative Arts Team, an American theatre in education company, was commissioned to conduct an artist-in-residency programme. The school is approximately a twenty-minute walk from the subway, and this walk takes you past abandoned homes, empty warehouses and boarded-up shops. The sound of traffic, and the thick stench of exhaust fumes, are forever constant as a busy freeway is close by. All of the conventional stereotypes of a ghetto were being demonstrated in front of me as I walked to the school on this first day, and I couldn't help but feel slightly on edge.

The ethnic breakdown was half Hispanic, half African American. These breakdowns are reflected in the elementary school where most of the 750 students live in single-parent families in the housing projects which surround the school.

The school is now named after a beloved former principal who was fatally shot as he went to find a student in the community. I was told that the principal was caught in crossfire, a result of a drug deal gone wrong.

When a colleague explained that Rustic was where Hubert Selby Jnr ([1957] 1988) set his book, *Last Exit to Brooklyn*, my anxiety increased for when this book first came out in the 1950s it caused quite a stir, given the moral deprivation, the violence, the prostitution, the despair and the agony depicted. 'A vision of hell' was how *The New York Times Book Review* described Selby's text. A recent book, *The Colour of Water* by James McBride (1997) was also about Rustic, describing how McBride grew up as one of thirteen black children with a white Jewish mother, and how he overcame poverty and other deprivations in the process. And *A View from the Bridge*, Arthur Miller's play, was set in Rustic, down at the dockyards, and became a disturbing portrait of domestic abuse and latent incest. So the area, Rustic, has received notoriety.

I was in the school because of my interest in tracking the circumstances which permit good reflective teaching in the arts, and the two teachers I was working with, let's call them Rachel and Minnie, were seen as potentially good case studies because they were about to plan and implement a drama lesson with the Creative Arts Team. I felt privileged to gain insight into how these teachers would go about using drama in their curriculum, and I'd like to highlight one aspect of their planning.

Rachel thought drama activity might be a good way to deal with the issue of stealing, an issue which she was concerned with in her own classroom. As she planned her lesson, she decided she would put her four- and five-year old children into role as an extended family of brothers and sisters who needed to go shopping to buy supplies for a birthday party. Rachel was going to play two roles. The first was as the older sister of the family who leads the shopping expedition. While shopping, this sister notices a doll on the floor of the shop, and decides to take it home with her. The second role, a role where the drama would put her children in a dilemma, was as a little girl with ponytails who had lost her doll in the shop. The little girl goes over to the big sister's house and asked the big sister if her doll was there. The children have to provide advice to the big sister, the teacher in role, as to whether or not she should give the doll back.

Minnie's planning started from another entry point. She had attended a drama workshop conducted by the arts agency, a workshop which had impressed her. 'We did this marvellous story', said Minnie, 'called Pip was afraid of the dark.' She described the workshop in her journal:

> *The workshop leader had props including a frog hat that she wore, and a large light blue piece of plastic for water. We were the froggies she was coming to visit. Pip had to travel through the forest to visit us. Fine, as long as it was daylight. When we started home it was dark and all the froggies had to come back with him through the dark forest. The workshop leader gave each of us a black piece of nylon to represent the night and she put music on and we danced to represent the dark (fast, slow, shimmering etc). Of course, Pip's mother was glad to see him when he arrived home. I plan to do this story in my class because I was so taken by it.*

Minnie was going to try and replicate her workshop experience. In her version of the drama, she was going to play Terry the turtle who was afraid of the dark, and the other children would play Terry's friends. The children go on a trip to help make Terry feel better, and on the way they meet two characters: a duck afraid of the water, and a lion afraid of loud noises. The roles of the duck and lion would be played by Minnie's assistant teachers.

Both Minnie's and Rachel's lessons were beautifully executed. The only props Rachel had were a wig with ponytails, which Rachel would wear to represent the little girl who had lost the doll, and a real doll with black ponytails which the elder sister took from the shop. Minnie, on the other hand, had gone to considerable effort preparing turtle hats, the water, a duck's outfit and a lion's lair.

The children in both classes had strong satisfying experiences. In Minnie's session, the children, in role as turtles, were taken on a journey through the forest where they encounter the duck and the lion. The children, with Terry, hear of these other animals' fears. The turtles finally go home and Terry had learned not to be afraid of the dark any more. In Rachel's class the children, who in role had told their sister to take the doll home, were challenged to rethink the appropriateness of this suggestion when they met the little girl who had lost her doll. Rachel went into role as the little girl to probe the children's responses, and to present them with an alternative way of looking at the world. Minnie's role work as Terry was more to lead the students through the narrative.

It was Minnie, though, who was the more disappointed of the two in how her lesson developed. 'The children just did what they were told', she wrote in her diary. 'I'm not happy with it, nothing much seemed to happen. It lacked a certain spark.' And to a certain extent there was some sense in what she was saying. The children had been led through a conventional plot, the details of which were known to the whole class in advance.

Minnie thought it would have been better had the children been more activated in their roles, perhaps helping Terry find ways that she could be less afraid of the dark. Also, rather than having the duck and lion tell the children what their fears were, perhaps the turtles could have tried to find this point out for themselves by encouraging the duck and lion to talk. Minnie's starting point, to create the props, was a different starting point from Rachel's. In Rachel's class it was the issue, stealing, that was a problem, and she thought drama was a way to deal with it.

Rachel helped the children actively commit to the drama, and it was the children's responses which would drive the work forward. If they thought it was a good idea for their sister to take the doll home, then they were being held accountable for their decision when the little girl came knocking on the door wanting her doll back. Rachel knew that the best kind of strategies to use in her drama were those which enabled the kids to ask the question, What is happening now? What action should I take? Is this action appropriate? The teacher in role then became an important distancing device to help reveal to the group the nature of their actions, and to question them on the possible implications of their actions. Minnie, being more arrested by detail, and by what is happening next in the drama (the turtles visit the duck, then they visit the lion, then they go home), wasn't interested in holding the moment up for scrutiny; rather, she wanted to give the children a good and satisfying playmaking experience.

I have drawn on this example because we can learn from Minnie's and Rachel's experiences as artist-educators. They have begun to reflect on how the arts operate as revelations of the world. They recognise that children need to be supported in their engagement with an artwork and that the teacher should be an active conspirator, if you like – one who assists the shaping and probing of the children's responses. But of equal interest to me is how both are prepared to explore how different artistic techniques can be incorporated into their curriculum. They both are open to examining their own praxis, gaining some distance from it, in order to understand what drives their thinking. Ironically, the more distance they gain, the greater understanding they have of the question, What is happening now?

3 Partnerships transform people

The theatre in education programme 'Who Cares?'[5] tracks the life of fifteen-year-old Sean as he becomes progressively more alienated from his family and friends. When Sean runs away from home, the student participants who observe 'Who Cares?' are enrolled as telephone counsellors in training for TEEN HELP, a youth hotline service for troubled teenagers who must advise Sean on his options. The student groups try and problem-solve what issues are raised for Sean, they hotseat him, and one another, they create images of Sean's dreams and fears, they thought-track the conflicts in his head, they construct a forum theatre scene of how he might lessen the stresses in his life.

This programme was piloted in a number of secondary school sites in Australia and involved a complex number of partnerships. There was the partnership between the tertiary students and their director as they worked over a four-week period to create the programme. The tertiary students came from two different institutions, so there was a further partnership between these universities. The Centre for Applied Theatre Research commissioned the project from a British director, so here was a further partnership between the commissioning agency and its artistic staff. And then there were partnerships been the schools who experienced the programme and the Centre. The actor-teachers were in partnership with the high school students, and the students were in partnership with each other, so the layering of partnerships in this example is multi-faceted.

Partnerships, when they work well, have the capacity to change people. As shown in the Regata example (pp. 120–122) they can help activate individuals to believe in their own capacity to wield and direct events; as well, then can open their eyes to different ways of conceiving of curriculum, as with the Rustic illustration. In the 'Who Cares?' partnership I was struck by how the actor-teachers were challenged to rethink the stereotypes they had created for themselves on schools and schooling. For many of these actor-teachers it was their first experience of a Theatre in Education programme, and through that experience they transformed their perceptions of teachers and teaching.

I well remember one school incident where these transformations were evident. We were working in a district, I'll call it Middletown, where teenage trauma was high. As Ball (1999) has argued, Australia has one of the highest rates of youth suicide in the world, and Queensland, where 'Who Cares?' was touring, consistently has very high rates. The team was exhausted on this particular day for they had worked in two schools in the morning, and had one more in the afternoon. It was towards the end of the school year, and the apathy of the school students seemed high, especially as we suspected that one reason for schools inviting us in was for us, the 'Who Cares?' company, to act as a time-filler, to provide some light entertainment for the students given that most of their final examinations and assessments had concluded.

We had trouble finding the afternoon school site as it was isolated from the main township. We had to drive down a deserted road for some kilometres before finding it. When we arrived we were met by the guidance officer who told us that we would be working with a group of Year Nine students (14–15-year-olds); the session would occur during their science class. It was, she explained, a 'problem class', predominantly 90 per cent male. As I asked her for further information, she said, 'Oh, you know, the school, it's got a reputation.'

'Surf culture', she continued, noticing my bewilderment. She looked at me and then pointed to a group of adolescent males with bleached hair. 'You know what I mean', she added. I stared at her blankly. 'That's one reason why I thought we have got to have you here. You're dealing with their problems, you'll help them. Sean and all of that.'

I noticed the anxiety of the actor-teachers rising. Not only was it the end of the school year where the actor-teachers themselves were exhausted, but we were hearing from this woman about a rambunctious group of surfies. As 'Who Cares?' was dependent on group interaction, I felt that the actor-teachers were now second guessing what such might entail with this negatively characterised school population. Seemingly ignorant of the actor-teachers' anxiety, the school counsellor proceeded: 'The kids have nothing to look forward to here, they have no home life, they are wild, the dole queue and surf look far more interesting to them than science today.'

'Do they know we are coming', I went on. 'Oh, I'm not sure', she replied.

I must concede that I, too, was feeling a little anxious, and wondered why I was there? 'It's important,' the school counsellor continued, 'that you finish in seventy minutes as the buses come to collect the students at 2.50 p.m. sharp.' I was amazed. All of the promotional material for 'Who Cares?' stated clearly that this programme required ninety minutes, and now, on top of everything else, we were being told to cut the time by twenty minutes.

As the actor-teachers went to set up the classroom space, the Year Nine students slowly began to appear, meandering to the room, having trouble listening to their supervisors say, 'Will you please line up.'

I called the actor-teachers together. 'Well, this is our last performance for the year. Let's make it our strongest.' I could read the fear on their faces. 'I think it would be a wonderful opportunity to work with this group, it's a science group, most of the time we are with drama classes. "Who Cares?" should be experienced by non-drama groups.'

And, to our surprise, the ninth-graders committed to the work from the outset, from the first minutes when they were enrolled as trainee counsellors for the telephone support service for teenagers in help. Yes, there were more males than we were used to, but in a sense this fuelled the work with tension as the students attempted to problem-solve how Sean, the fifteen-year-old male runaway, might deal effectively with the circumstances which oppress him.

It did seem like the Sean scenario was resonating with the group. Using techniques like hotseating Sean, the students were provided with opportunities to question him and to make suggestions as to how he might manage his life circumstances. In one stage of the programme, as the students watch Sean interact with his mother and his two younger sisters, at a moment in Sean's life where he realises the growing responsibilities that will be placed upon him at home, the students take turns at assuming the role of Sean. They roleplay different ways he might interact with his family. We were later told that two of the male students who took on the role of Sean had been threatened with expulsion from the school on numerous occasions.

For the actor-teachers, working at this particular site on this day, challenged them to rethink the stereotypes they had of schools and schooling. In a real sense, they had transformed their own prejudices as they artfully partnered themselves as actor-teachers with the student participants.

In these final reflections from the actor-teachers on the programme, they comment on the changes that took place within themselves through the partnership. In this first example, the teaching artist contemplates how conventional notions of academic excellence seem odd when working with the Middletown school:

> For myself this was my most favourite show. The students in the audience were all Seans and for some reason Sean's problems were nothing compared to their own. But these kids had spark. We had been warned that these students were all of a low academic ability, but WHO CARES? deals with life, not ability so the students were all equal when they walked in the door. This show also demonstrated that the more personal problems the students have, the more they can

bring to the show. The one student who was really participating I later learnt was on the border line of being expelled from the school because of his behaviour and academic standing. WHO CARES? strongly demonstrates that these at risk students can't excel in maths or science, but when it comes to life experiences they go to the head of the class. The students don't have academic problems they just have bigger problems in their home life than they do at school.

In this next example, an actor-teacher reflects on how the partnership liberates participants to understand their world and their own role in its evolution:

❝ *This group of students I believe was the best and most rewarding group we have ever worked with. They allowed us to come back together and understand the aims and benefits of WHO CARES? It inspired us to continue and see the demand for this kind of work, as we saw how young adults are ill prepared socially, mentally and physically to become adults in this fast changing world. As McLaren states, 'an understanding of the language of self can help better nego-tiate the world. It can also help us begin to forge the basis of social transformation: the building of a better world, the altering of the very ground which we live and work.' WHO CARES? initiates this kind of learning as the programme aims to build a place for young adults to actively participate and build their awareness of self which I believe and have seen awakens their consciousness. Thus, as Boal advocates, 'theatre becomes a tool that is not revolutionary in itself, but is surely a rehearsal for the revolution.'*

These actor-teachers are young adults, our future educational leaders, who are beginning to recognise the power of innovative partnerships, especially when these partnerships are managed well. Like the examples from Regata School, and the one in Rustic, and the above illustration from Middletown, we are observing how drama praxis:

■ activates teachers and students to believe in their own worth
■ enables participants to reflect on the question, What is happening now?
■ transforms people's understanding of their world

And it is the praxis, and the partnerships which emerge from it, that can liberate educators to examine their curriculum and themselves in new ways.

Notes

1 This symposium was the subject for a special issue of *NJ* (*NADIE Journal*, the national journal of Drama Australia) which focused on aesthetic education. See *NJ*, Volume 23, Number 2.

2 Maxine Greene expressed this view at the School Reform through the Arts, an international seminar with David Best, Maxine Greene, and Madeleine Grumet, Creative Arts Team, New York University, 19 June 1998. See *Applied Theatre Researcher*, a new electronic journal published by the Centre for Applied Theatre Research at Griffith University. Website address: www.gu.edu.au/centre/atr

3 See ibid. for source.

4 Rustic, like the names of other schools and their districts in this chapter, is a pseudonym. However, the executive director of the Creative Arts Team (CAT) at New York University, Lynda Zimmerman, and the artistic director, Christopher Vine, were pleased for the arts agency to be named in this book.

5 This programme was commissioned by the Centre for Applied Theatre Research at Griffith University from the Language Alive company in Birmingham, England. The director of Language Alive, Dr Steve Ball (1999), was in residence at the Centre when the programme was devised.

References

BECKERMAN, B. (1970) *Dynamics of Drama*, New York: Knopf.

BALL, S. (1999) 'Playing on the margins: creating safe spaces through the arts', *NJ*, **23**, 2, pp. 28–32.

BOLTON, G. (1979) *Towards a Theory of Drama in Education*, Harlow: Longman.

BOLTON, G. (1998) *Acting in Classroom Drama: A Critical Analysis*, Stoke-on-Trent: Trentham Books.

FREIRE, P. (1970) *Pedagogy of the Oppressed*, New York: Continuum.

McBRIDE, J. (1997) *The Colour of Water*, Rydalmere, New South Wales: Sceptre.

MERKIN, D. (1999) 'Scoundrel time', *The New Yorker*, 4 October, pp. 110–111.

O'NEILL, C. (1995) *Drama Worlds: A Framework for Process Drama*, Portsmonth, N.H.: Heinemann.

SELBY, H. ([1957] 1988) *Last Exit to Brooklyn*, New York: Grove Press.

Resources and further reading

For the beginner wanting to introduce drama praxis in the curriculum

Ball, C. and Ayrs, J. (1995) *Taking Time to Act: A Guide to Cross-Curricular Drama*, Portsmouth, N.H.: Heinemann.
A good introduction to some of the core strategies drama teachers need to develop. While informed from a British perspective, it breaks down many of the negative stereotypes of drama in a whole-school context.

Booth, D. (1994) *Story Drama: Reading, Writing and Roleplaying Across the Curriculum*, Markham, Ontario: Pembroke Publishers.
This volume presents an anecdotal description of the progress and development of David Booth's teaching philosophy and method of incorporating storydrama into all aspects of classroom learning.

Booth, D. (1994) *Classroom Voices: Language-Based Learning in the Elementary School*, Toronto: Harcourt, Brace & Company.
A guide and resource for teachers of language arts which presents current educational theory in balance with examples, anecdotes and discussions of real-school examples of application and balance.

Booth, D. and Barton, B. (1990) *Stories in the Classroom: Storytelling, Reading Aloud and Role-playing with Children*, Markham, Ontario: Pembroke and Heinemann.
A collaboration between two leading storytellers/teachers, this book is a valuable guide for teachers looking for new approaches to bringing children and stories together.

Booth, D. and Lundy, C. (1985) *Improvisation*, Toronto: Academic Press.
An excellent teachers' handbook which covers the variety of strategies and techniques open to the process drama worker. Numerous activities suggested.

Bunyan, P. and Rainer, J. (1996) *The Patchwork Quilt: A Cross-phase Educational Drama Project*, Sheffield: National Association for the Teaching of English.
A cross-phase educational project built around a series of encounters between an elderly woman and her past. Pitched for the top junior and early secondary years.

Burgess, R. and Gaudry, P. (1995) *Time for Drama: A Handbook for Secondary Teachers*, Milton Keynes: Longman Cheshire.
Written by Australian authors, this text provides many practical ideas for drama teachers within a sound theoretical framework. It aims to satisfy teachers' needs for drama activities but also to provide a comprehensive consideration of the dramatic process.

Burton, B. (1995) *Making Drama: A Course for Junior Secondary Students*, South Melbourne: Longman.
Focused on the skills and knowledge for the junior secondary level that is at the core of the Australian curriculum.

Burton, B. (1996) *Creating Drama: A Drama Course for Middle Secondary Students*, South Melbourne: Longman.
Designed to provide teachers and students in the middle school with a complete drama course based on Australian curriculum.

Clipson-Boyles, S. (1998) *Drama in Primary School Teaching*, London: David Fulton.
This book provides primary school teachers with drama opportunities for their students as required by the National Curriculum Order for English in the UK.

Fines, J. and Verriour, R. (1974) *The Drama of History*, London: New University Education.
One of the first books specifically written on the relationship between process drama and the history curriculum. These English authors examine how the work of Dorothy Heathcote might open up the world of English history.

Fleming, M. (1994) *Starting Drama Teaching*, London: David Fulton.
Each chapter in this excellent introductory text contains examples of specific lessons, from which insights into the aims and purposes of drama are derived. Current controversies are addressed, and a comprehensive guide to the published literature is provided.

Fleming, M. (1997) *The Art of Drama Teaching*, London: David Fulton.
Discusses twenty-five drama techniques, each accompanied by practical examples of lessons and illustrated by an extract from a play. Explores how dramatic form is demonstrated in playtext and process drama.

Fox, M. (1987) *Teaching Drama to Young Children*, Portsmouth, N.H.: Heinemann.
Written for teachers of children aged five to eight who would like to teach drama but are not sure of how to begin. The author gives specific instructions on how to set up activities in which children can develop imagination, confidence and language growth.

Haseman, B. and O'Toole, J. (1986) *Dramawise: An Introduction to the Elements of Drama*, Richmond: Heinemann Educational Australia.
The activities, role-plays and improvisations are addressed directly to the middle secondary school student. A text widely used in Australia and the UK.

Haseman, B. and O'Toole, J. (1990) *Communicate Live! Exploring the Functions of Spoken Language*, Port Melbourne: Heinemann.
This text explores the links between spoken, dramatic and written language and communication.

Heathcote, D. and Bolton, G. (1995) *Drama for Learning: Dorothy Heathcote's Mantle of the Expert Approach to Education*, Portsmouth, N.H.: Heinemann.
A thorough discussion of Heathcote's innovative mantle of the expert approach. Starting with a problem or task, teachers and students explore, in role, the knowledge they already have while making new discoveries along the way. This book is part of the 'Dimensions of Drama' series (Heinemann publications, USA; editor Cecily O'Neill).

Johnson, L. and O'Neill, C. (eds) (1984) *Dorothy Heathcote: Collected Writings on Education and Drama*, London: Heinemann.
The editors have collected many of the most influential Heathcote papers which cover her approach to education and learning. An important volume for those interested in probing Heathcote's praxis.

Kitson, N. and Spiby, I. (1997) *Drama 7–11: Developing Primary Teaching Skills*, London: Routledge.
The authors propose a curriculum for drama that combines the diverse references in the various documents of the National Curriculum in the UK.

Manley, A. and O'Neill, C. (1997) *Dreamseekers: Creative Approaches to the African American Heritage*, Portsmouth, N.H.: Heinemann.
Examines significant African-American themes and how they can be addressed through drama and role-play. A range of teachers contribute their curriculum ideas.

Marson, P., Brockbank, K., McGuire, B. and Morton, S. (1990) *Drama 14–16: A book of Projects and Resources*, Cheltenham: Stanley Thornes.
Offers ten thematic units with an emphasis on interaction and improvisation, but includes written assignments, discussion and study of dramatic texts. Geared into National Curriculum developments in the UK.

Moore, T. (ed.) (1998) *Phoenix Texts: A Window on Drama Practice in
    Australian Primary Schools*, Brisbane: Drama Australia Publications.
Explores how seven Australian primary school teachers develop a drama
from the same pre-text.

Morgan, N. and Saxton, J. (1987) *Teaching Drama: A Mind of Many Wonders*,
    London: Hutchinson.
A popular Canadian handbook for all drama teachers written in an accessible
plain style. Each chapter focuses on one skill – its advantages, how to use it,
problems and solutions, grounded examples and skill-building exercises for
the teacher to consolidate the learning.

Neelands, J. (1984) *Making Sense of Drama*, Oxford: Heinemann.
Applies the thinking of leaders in drama praxis into practical plans.

Neelands, J. (1998) *Beginning Drama 11–14*, London: David Fulton.
Written to fit National Curriculum Guidelines in England, the text provides
an accessible account of what teachers need to know and do in order to
teach effectively.

Neelands, J. (edited by Tony Goode) (1990) *Structuring Drama Work:
    A Handbook of Available Forms in Theatre and Drama*, Cambridge:
    Cambridge University Press.
A practical handbook for drama teachers and youth theatre workers. It offers
a range of theatrical conventions to help initiate, focus and develop dramatic
activity.

O'Neill, C. and Lambert, A. (1982) *Drama Structures: A Practical Handbook
    for Beginners*, London: Hutchinson.
An influential text on how process drama is experienced by students. Each
of the lessons documented has been taught with students, and the authors
demonstrate the kind of choices open to teachers given the responses of the
group.

O'Neill, C., Lambert, A., Linnell, R. and Warr-Wood, J. (1976) *Drama
    Guidelines*, London: Heinemann.
An earlier shorter version of *Drama Structures* which introduces the key
principles which inform process drama. A non-threatening collection of
activities are proposed for the beginning teacher.

Readman, G. and Lamont, G. (1994) *Drama*, London: BBC Educational
    Publishing.
Written essentially for the British non-specialist primary school teacher,
numerous suggestions for planning, implementation and assessment are
provided, as well as how drama might facilitate national educational
priorities.

Rohd, M. (1998) *Theatre for Community, Conflict and Dialogue: The Hope is
    Vital Training Manual*, Portsmouth, N.H.: Heinemann.

Provides advice on how to give opportunities for young people to open up and explore their feelings through theatre, offering a safe place for them to air their views with dignity, respect and freedom.

Saldaña, J. (1995) *Drama of Colour: Improvisation with Multiethnic Folklore*, Portsmouth, N.H.: Heinemann.
A good resource for using drama to enhance young children's ethnic literacy by provoking personal insights into our multiethnic world.

Somers, J. (1994) *Drama in the Curriculum*, London: Cassell.
Written for teachers involved with the National Curriculum in England, this text shows how drama might enhance the learning potential of students.

Sternberg, P. (1998) *Theatre for Conflict Resolution: In the Classroom and Beyond*, Portsmouth, N.H.: Heinemann.
Outlines a variety of playmaking activities and theatre games designed to teach students that drama can bring together diverse people and points of view.

Swartz, L. (1995) *Dramathemes*, Portsmouth, N.H.: Heinemann.
Written by a popular Canadian elementary school teacher, this text is an excellent introduction to drama in the classroom, and provides a structured thematic approach towards lesson planning and implementation. Teachers love this book.

Tarlington, C. and Verriour, P. (1983) *Offstage: Elementary Education through Drama*, Toronto: Oxford University Press.
This book addresses itself to the generalist elementary teacher, providing suggestions for integration into other areas of the curriculum, especially Language Arts and Social Studies.

Taylor, P. (ed.) (1995) *Pre-text and Storydrama: The Artistry of Cecily O'Neill and David Booth*, Brisbane: National Association for Drama in Education (available from the Drama Australia Office, c/o NADIE Administrator, PO Box 163, Albert St, Brisbane QLD 4002 Australia).
A short monograph which examines two key aspects of process drama which have been developed by the field's leaders: pre-text and storydrama. The monograph follows the practice of O'Neill and Booth and includes the responses of teachers and the students to process drama.

Taylor, P. (1998) *Redcoats and Patriots: Reflective Practice in Drama and Social Studies*, Portsmouth, N.H.: Heinemann.
An introduction to how drama might be layered into the social studies curriculum. The text is grounded in experiences with Grade Seven students. Published as part of the 'Dimensions of Drama' Series by Heinemann.

Warren, B. (1996) *Drama Games: Drama and Group Activities for Leaders Working with People of All Ages and Abilities*, North York, Ontario: Captus Press.

This very practical and popular book contains many easy-to-use and well-tested games and role-playing activities for people who work with groups.

Winston, J. and Tandy, M. (1998) *Beginning Drama 4–11*, London: David Fulton.
Provides a positive and accessible account of what primary school teachers need to know, understand and be able to do in order to ensure that their first experiences of drama are controlled and effective.

Woolland, B. (1993) *The Teaching of Drama in the Primary School*, London: Longman.
An excellent book which introduces process drama to the elementary school teacher. While informed by policies developed in the British National Curriculum, and how process drama might achieve key attainment levels, the book will be accessible to teachers elsewhere.

Resources on drama praxis for the informed

Bolton, G. (1979) *Towards a Theory of Drama in Education*, London: Longman.
One of the first works on how process drama is different from other modes of drama activity in schools. Bolton proposes four types of drama, and then outlines why type four (drama for learning) is a powerful educative tool.

Bolton, G. (1984) *Drama in Education*, London: Longman.
Bolton takes the reader through some of the major historical emphases on the development of process drama, and makes a compelling case as to why drama should be at the centre of the curriculum.

Bolton, G. (1992) *New Perspectives on Classroom Drama*, Hemel Hempstead: Simon & Schuster.
Bolton updates some of his earlier theories on classroom drama, exploring with greater clarity the nexus between artistry and practice, and includes a series of lessons for all ages.

Bolton, G. (1998) *Acting in Classroom Drama: A Critical Analysis*, Stoke-on-Trent: Trentham Books.
Written by one of the foremost authorities on drama education for children and young people, this penetrating text analyses the theory, practice and evaluation of classroom drama.

Booth, D. (1987) *Drama Words: The Role of Drama in Language Growth*, Toronto: Language Study Centre, Toronto Board of Education.
An important study on the relationship between drama and language. Booth explores how the intentions of the language teacher can be supported by the process drama worker. This book is an excellent resource for language specialists interested in drama.

Booth, D. and Martin-Smith, A. (eds) (1988) *Re-cognising Richard Courtney*, Markham, Ontario: Pembroke.
A collection of articles which represent Professor Richard Courtney's effect on drama internationally.

Booth, D. and Neelands, J. (eds) (1998) *Writing in Role: Classroom Projects Connecting Writing and Drama*, Hamilton, Ontario: Caliburn Enterprises.
This book is a collection of classroom projects in which the teacher and the students, often in partnership with a university mentor, engage in units of exploration that incorporate dramatic and written expression to facilitate learning.

Byron, K. (1986) *Drama in the English Curriculum*, New York: Methuen.
A cleverly constructed text, written as a series of journal entries between a beginning and experienced teacher. The focus is on how drama can be introduced into the language arts curriculum. Numerous examples of using drama to explore text are provided.

Davis, D. and Lawrence, C. (eds) (1986) *Gavin Bolton: Selected Writings*, London: Longman.
A comprehensive selection of twenty-six of the best and most useful of Gavin Bolton's papers, articles and essays. Subjects covered include: the nature of children's drama, drama and emotion, implications for drama as an artform, and drama and teaching/learning.

Heathcote, D. (1980) *Drama as Context*, Aberdeen: National Association for the Teaching of English.
Part One describes the Ozymandias Saga, a project on the theme of conquest, which was undertaken with children in a Newcastle (UK) primary school. Part Two describes an experiment in teacher education in which Heathcote demonstrated an approach to text which was designed to deepen understanding of Brecht's play *Caucasian Chalk Circle* and the role of the teacher in the classroom.

Hodgson, J. and Richards, E. ([1966] 1974) *Improvisation*, New York: Grove Press.
Examines how improvisation can be understood, harnessed and developed, not only in theatre but in therapy and in education.

Hornbrook, D. (1989) *Education in Drama: Casting the Dramatic Curriculum*, London: Falmer.
Provides a theoretical case on why drama must be taught as a performing arts subject.

Hornbrook, D. (1998) *Education and Dramatic Art* (2nd edn), London: Routledge.
A contentious attempt to critique the praxis of Heathcote and Bolton. Regrettably, this second edition does not advance the debate, and it ignores the widespread criticisms of the author's first edition.

Hornbrook, D. (ed.) (1998) *On the Subject of Drama*, London: Routledge.
A collection of drama specialists claim how drama should be taught as an arts subject.

Hughes, C. (1998) *Museum Theatre: Communicating with Visitors through Drama*, Portsmouth, N.H.: Heinemann.
Opens up the power of live theatre in museum settings.

McArdle, J. (1998) *Flying on Both Wings: A Theory of Drama and Theatre in Education* (Pamphlet), The National Theatre: The Outreach Programme Pamphlet Series Number 1, Dublin, The Outreach Programme of the National Theatre.
A leading Irish educator outlines a theory of drama and theatre in education.

McGregor, L., Tate, M. and Robinson, K. (1977) *Learning through Drama*, London: Heinemann.
This text examines the distinctive contribution drama can make to the curriculum and is informed by a national research and development project sponsored by the Schools Council in the UK.

McLean, J. (1996) *An Aesthetic Framework in Drama: Issues and Implications*, Brisbane: Drama Australia Publications.
This research monograph, the second paper in the NADIE Research Monograph Series, demystifies the aesthetic and encourages teachers to develop their own aesthetic consciousness in order to place confidently the aesthetic at the centre of their drama teaching.

Miller, C. and Saxton, J. (eds) (1999) *Drama and Theatre in Education: International Conservations*, Victoria, British Columbia: The American Educational Research Association and the International Drama in Education Research Institute.
A series of papers which represent the research and practice of over thirty drama educators from around the world.

Muir, A. (1996) *New Beginnings: Knowledge and Form in the Drama of Bertolt Brecht and Dorothy Heathcote*, Stoke-on-Trent: Trentham Books.
This monograph forms part of a series of works on education from the University of Central England. Muir focuses on Brecht and Heathcote, contrasting their knowledge of human understanding and dramatic form.

O'Neill, C. (1995) *Drama Worlds: A Framework for Process Drama*, Portsmouth, N.H.: Heinemann.
Considers process drama's sources and its connections with more familiar kinds of improvisation: the text it generates, the kinds of roles available, its relation to the audience and dramatic time, and the leader's function in the event. Many examples of process dramas provided. This is the first book in the 'Dimensions of Drama' series (Heinemann; general editor Cecily O'Neill).

O'Toole, J. (1992) *The Process of Drama: Negotiating Art and Meaning*,
    London: Routledge.
Explores the relationships between the playwright, the elements of dramatic
art, and the other artists involved in the process of drama. Areas covered
include the dramatic context; roles and relationships; the drama space;
language, movement and gesture; tension and the audience.

O'Toole, J. and Donelan, K. (1996) *Drama, Culture and Empowerment:
    The IDEA Dialogues*, Brisbane: IDEA Publications.
Papers which emerged from the Third International Drama/Theatre and
Education Association Congress.

Peter, M. (1995) *Making Drama Special: Developing Drama Practice to Meet
    Special Educational Needs*, London: David Fulton.
Presents a practical guide for developing reflective drama practice in relation
to pupils with learning difficulties, taking account of the particular pressures
presented by such challenging teaching situations.

Somers, J. (1996) *Drama and Theatre in Education: Contemporary Research*,
    North York, Ontario: Captus.
Papers presented at a research conference at the University of Exeter in 1995.

Taylor, P. (ed.) (1996) *Researching Drama and Arts Education: Paradigms
    and Possibilities*, London: Falmer.
A handbook which covers the variety of research methods open to
investigators of drama praxis.

Taylor, P. & Hoepper, C. (eds) (1995) *Selected Readings in Drama and
    Theatre Education*, Brisbane: NADIE Publications.
The chapters in this book present the richness and diversity of arts praxis
offered to delegates at the 1995 Congress of the International Drama/Theatre
and Education Association.

Wagner, B. J. (1998) *Educational Drama and Language Arts: What Research
    Shows*, Portsmouth, N.H.: Heinemann.
A summary of research on drama in education and creative drama, featuring
studies that show drama's effect on thinking, oral language, reading and
writing.

Wagner, B. J. (1999) *Dorothy Heathcote: Drama as a Learning Medium*
    (revised edn), Portland, Me.: Calender Islands Publishers.
Given that Heathcote has not authored a book alone, Wagner's documentation
of her evolving practice in the early 1970s is an important contribution to
the field. While Heathcote's ideas shifted markedly from the time when this
book was first published in 1976, the power of her work is clearly apparent,
and some of the key principles which informed her early practice are
outlined in this revised edition.

Wagner, B. J. (ed.) (1999) *Building Moral Communities through Educational Drama*, Stamford, Conn.: Ablex Publishing Corporation.
This book examines the way drama can bring about effective character education. It shows what happens when drama is used to deepen understanding of human affairs.

Warren, B. (ed.) (1995) *Creating a Theatre in your Classroom*, North York, Ontario: Captus Press.
Explores problems and concerns in the training of drama educators and in the practice of educational drama.

Wilhelm, J. and Edmiston, B. (1998) *Imagining to Learn: Inquiry, Ethics and Integration through Drama*, Portsmouth, N.H.: Heinemann.
This text demonstrates how drama taps into the imagination to create powerful learning contexts.

Winston, J. (1998) *Drama, Narrative and Moral Education*, London: Falmer Press.
Based on the author's doctoral thesis, this book provides a fascinating insight into the links between narrative, drama and moral education.

Index